Sophie Braka lives in Cheshire and is a qualified lawyer, she currently practises as a Pro Bono lawyer.

In her spare time she loves reading thriller novels, writing diaries and walking her little dancing Chihuahua, Stan.

This book is dedicated to my late father, Jack Braka, and my mum, Josie Braka, and to my beautiful, amazing daughter, Charlotte Braka.

SOPHIE LUCY BRAKA

1984 – DIARY OF A 16/17-YEAR-OLD

AUSTIN MACAULEY PUBLISHERS[TM]

LONDON • CAMBRIDGE • NEW YORK • SHARJAH

A CIP catalogue record for this title is available from the British Library.

ISBN 9781398486614 (Paperback)
ISBN 9781398486621 (ePub e-book)

www.austinmacauley.com

First Published 2022
Austin Macauley Publishers Ltd®
1 Canada Square
Canary Wharf
London
E14 5AA

I would like to thank the wonderful Dawn Paula Hockenhull (my typist) and Techno type (for all my printing and copying needs).

Chapter 1

December 1983 – January 1984

Monday 26th December 1983

Today I stayed at home because last night (Xmas Day) I was out with Charlotte and Co and I was tired. I did not do any work, so lazy!! I exercised though, outside with Dad's Walkman up and down the path for half an hour. Then I watched TV and tried to get an early night to recover from being out on Wed 21st, Thurs 22nd, Friday 23rd. Antonia and Graham and Granny came round for dinner. 24th we went to Allpark to celebrate Martin getting into Cambridge.

Tuesday 27th December 1983

Today I got up early and had a shower and washed my hair. I then went to Didsbury to Ric Michael's house where he was having a small party for ten people. Tanya, Carmella and Tez, Tim, Mike, Sarah, Rob, Louise, were all there and lots of booze. Had an okay time apart from being bored for quite a while. Went at about 6 o'clock as did not want to stay to go to a party in Northenden which Ric had invited me to as I was too tired. Glad to be home, I enjoyed watching Dallas – ace, and then I watched some Thriller Story. There was a Harefield do at Bennetts – but did not go – no ticket.

Wednesday 28th December 1983

Today I got up quite late as I was very tired. I started to get ready to go to Manchester. I said I would be there at 2.15 p.m. but by the time I was ready and we had to go to Wilmslow he was gone when I called at 3 o'clock. Very disappointed I was after all just thinking! Then I got on the train and went to Manchester. Bought some things for school i.e. socks, shirt and a few other things. On Friday 30th I bought some great stationery in the sale at Lewis's including this diary. Came back from town totally knackered and watched TV for the rest of the night.

Thursday 29th December 1983

Today I stayed in all day and actually got some work done which is incredible for me. I did some Pure Maths, which took up most of the afternoon (it was copying up as well!!). Then I phoned Charlotte twice and she invited me out tomorrow night with her. I watched TV. Mainly Top of The Pops and then Coronation Street. Exercised on Bike. Dad went to Lanzarote for one week today with Henry.

Friday 30th December 1983

Today I woke up and washed my hair and had a shower and then I went to the dermatologist (Dr August) in Knutsford about my skin. He gave me some stuff. Then went to Knutsford centre and looked at In Wear stuff. V. nice. Saw Francesca there. Then I went to town with Simon and Fran in car and got train back. Bought two tops and a new school coat (£20) from Miss Selfridge. I then got ready to go for dinner at Aunty. Monica's new house on Brook Lane.

Sarah and David were there and had a super time. Lovely vegetarian meal and saw Aunty. Monica's beautiful house. Talked and thought David was a very nice person and really sexy. Lucky Sarah. Sarah also looked very nice.

Started spot, tablets from Doctor's

Saturday 31st December 1983

Woke up at 12.30p.m. I did a bit of homework – Pure Maths but was not v. successful. Phoned Charlotte and then went to a party in Alderley Edge – it was really good – Chaz, Nick, Ric Goddard, all the Wilmslow lot including Billy etc. Robbie Lyne, Christine, Ailsa, Eleanor, Anna, Maggey, William Rosen, Andrew Cusworth, Ed Jackson. I went with Tez Livingstone from Manchester Grammar School (MGS) and he asked me out! I really like him. Bit spotty though.

Period started

Sunday 1st January 1984

Today I woke up at 1 o'clock. Just shows how knackered I am. Anyway as usual wasted most of my afternoon watching TV and then I did a bit of work. Mum, Ivan and Martin all went to Granny's for lunch. Tez (i.e. Terence L) phoned me, had a nice chat and then Ric, Michael phoned to invite me to a party on Monday 2nd (Gary Leons). I agreed but I don't really want to invite Tez along – wary!!

Monday 2nd January 1984

Today I woke up late and had a big breakfast. I did some work in the afternoon (Pure Maths) and I was v. bored. Did not do any exercising at all today. Sammy Chadwick phoned me of course only for a lift back from a party in Didsbury, why else but for a use? Anyway, got ready for the party and went to Sammy's house where Jackie, Liz, Kate and Sammy were. Got lift to Gary Leon's house. Good party i.e. met nice boy called Neil Jackson. Talked to Jenny Mersey. Lucy Braka was there. Rick was there, Tim and Lara, Kaz, Carmel etc. Everybody got to know about me and Tez Livingstone?!!

Tuesday 3rd January 1984

I had an appointment today at 10.30 p.m. but of course I woke up very late which resulted in Mum and me rushing to the Knutsford Hospital for my blood test. I went for my blood test and was glad to get it over and done with and came home and had breakfast. Today I did a tiny bit of homework and exercised on my bike. Must do more daily exercise. Then we watched Dallas and I had my dinner and then I watched American Cowboy which was crap. Today, I arranged to get the coach to school in the mornings instead of the train because then I don't have to face this weather.

Wednesday 4th January 1984

Today I got up quite late and had my breakfast. I did some homework (i.e. Pure Maths) for this horrible test I am going to get and I also watched quite a bit of TV. I exercised twice on my bicycle (10 minutes total) and went for a twenty-minute brisk walk along our path. Then I did some stretch exercises to keep me supple. I then had a shower and washed my hair. I got organised for school tomorrow and set my alarm for 7 a.m. Dead early hey? Well I have to discipline myself because now I'm catching the coach. I went to bed at 11 o'clock after catching a bit of Whicker's World on TV.

Thursday 5th January 1984

Today it was my first day back at school. I didn't get a wink of sleep last night probably because of school. Anyway, when I got up at 7 o'clock I was frazzled out. I had to be ready by 8 o'clock to leave for the coach at 8.10 a.m. I caught the coach and spoke to Laura. Then I went to form period and then to the library where I talked to Tim. Then I had double Maths, and then after to the common room and then to lunch. At recess Rick Michael took the piss out of my big nose. I had double Economics next, then I went to the library for some hist. books. Got train to Wilmslow – did some shopping in Wilmslow with Mum. Then exercised outside (15 minutes) two times on a bike. Spoke to Tez on the phone, seeing him on Saturday (mentioned my exercising) went to bed at 12 o'clock!

Friday 6th January 1984

Today, I decided to have a lie in as I have triple free at school. I woke up at 9.30 a.m. and got ready for school. I was late of course for my first lesson and I was very annoyed. Anyway got into the common room and had a good time talking to people. Had one lesson of History which was a relief and then I went back to the common room. Stuart said he fancied me but he talks a load of crap. After school I went to Knutsford.

Was invited to Nate Eccles' party tonight, but decided not to go. Danny Shineman phoned me – had a good chat, and like a fool stayed up until 1 o'clock watching a shit film "Play Misty for Me".

Saturday 7th January 1984

Today, I stayed in all day as it was freezing outside and I couldn't go to town. I got ready to meet Tez in my In Wear clothes and did not feel good. I met him in the Bleedin Wolf with Danny and Jim. We went on to The Griffin where John was, Miki Belcher, Adam Carr etc. I felt all night that Tez didn't partake like me, and I wasn't too keen on him. We went to a party in Hale where Tom, Jane, Natalie, Gillian, etc. were. Then off to Manchester Airport – which was okay. Jim gave me a lift home.

Sunday 8th January 1984

Today I got up late and did a bit of work. Tom phoned me and he asked me to see his house. Dad hurt his thigh falling off his bike and Dr Kennison came round. Charlotte and Melanie and Clare Stafford came round to see me to go to The Plough but left as it was not open. Then Tom came at 7 p.m. and took me to his house which is really amazing (v. luxurious) beautiful in fact. I really like Tom and his gorgeous car. Then watched The Thombirds which was quite good. Went to bed at 11 o'clock.

Monday 9th January 1984

Today I had to get up at 7 o'clock for school. I was ready by 8 o'clock but Martin delayed me and I thought that I had missed the bus, but fortunately I had not. It was absolutely freezing today. I had my first History lesson with Mr Freer. People took the mickey out of my big nose again. When I got home I exercised on the bike and did 15 minutes exercise outside. Then I had a shower and washed my hair and went to Young Enterprise which was extremely boring (got £15 to get the stuff). I got home, watched The Thombirds. Tez phoned me, then Jenny Mesri phoned me and we had a good chat. Went to bed at 11.30 p.m. which is extremely late – must go earlier in future.

Tuesday 10th January 1984

Today I caught the coach to school and talked to Tracey Wickens. 1 had double Oxbridge History (which was okay) and then I had double History. I thought that I was not going to get through the day, it was going so slowly. Then I had dinner and I had a fattening pudding.

Then I had double Maths. I went to Manchester after school where I got Benetton culottes (£18.90) and some pink exercise tights for Discourse tomorrow. I got home at 7.30 p.m. after seeing Mandy Alywood at the station. I watched Dallas and tidied my bedroom up. I didn't do any work tonight and I didn't do any work last night. I must get working tomorrow night after school. I didn't exercise at all. I was just too lazy to work tonight, I just read on the floor in my chamber.

Wednesday 11th January 1984

Today I caught the bus again and as usual Martin was being a real bastard to me in the car on the way there. I spoke to Francesca – what a pain! Anyway, morning lessons were okay. Got a feeling today that I am going to give up Oxbridge in the near future (Gillian Cohen is not doing it). Went to Discourse and I felt a real fat slob. I have put on a lot of weight and I must get it off. After this I got the train home. I did some Pure Maths homework today and then exercised outside (15 minutes) and had a shower and washed my hair. Watched TV and Whicker's World while trying to do some work. I went to bed at 11.20 p.m. last night. I went to bed at 11.00 p.m. I think.

Thursday 12th January 1984

Today, I caught the coach and saw Vicki Price who looked v. pretty. I had an okay morning with double Maths and lunch time though I had an annoying time at dinner. Kat, Faz, Gill, Lara, Sarah and Andy were all taking the piss out of me, stealing my food etc. I got rather emotional (tears in my eyes) and felt a real stiff. Sarah enjoyed it of course! Anyway, by the way, it was Kate Whitehead's birthday today. Got through the afternoon okay, did a bit of Pure Maths prep but hardly any really to what I wanted to do. Watched Top of the Pops (referred to as T.O.T.P) and Charlotte phoned me at 9–9.30 p.m. Anyway, then I watched a Health Farm programme and just lazed about til 11.20. I went to bed at 11.50 p.m. which is too late.

Friday 13th January 1984 (Charlotte's Birthday)

Today, it was absolutely freezing, it was very windy indeed and rainy. I talked to Vicki Price before the bus and then Cath Hadfield on the bus who told me about the practices for the tennis team next term. Had the Pure Maths test which I made a hash up of. After school went to town with Mum. We went to the jeweller's where we got Chari and Sam's (Xmas) presents and then went to Fred Aldous for some other things and then on to Dorothy Perkins for tights. Got home, had dinner, watched TV. Phoned Danny (out). Had a chat with Tez on the phone. Charlotte did not phone back. Watched a good film called "The 12 Angry Men" with Henry Fonda which was excellent, but didn't get to bed til 2 o'clock which is terrible.

Saturday 14th January 1984

Today I stayed in all day and did not do any work. At 9.30 p.m. I set off for Robin Huton and Phil Copeland's 18th Party in Altrincham and I got there at 10 p.m. Everybody was there including Danny (who I really fancy). I saw Tez and went with him. Saw Vicki Abadi there and had a chat. Sarah, Jo Ingleby, Henry, Liza Mesri, Natalie, Alexis, Danielle and Andy, Jim gave me a lift home and got to bed at 2.45 a.m. Tom phoned today as well. Love him.

Sunday 15th January 1984

I woke up at 12 o'clock today and had breakfast. I would not work probably because of Ivan who had come back from Oxford; in fact I did no work. I was v. depressed, listened to the radio. I phoned Charlotte and we had a little argument about Tez (I don't know why I am going out with him? He is ugly). Then I watched The Thornbirds and went to bed at 10.40 p.m. Got school tomorrow so must get some sleep.

What To Put on UCCA? 1984

- Young Enterprise – Managing Director
- Member of Jewish Societies – "Shekels" and "Koach" – Discos
- Tennis Team —> members and player for A E C C.
- Dance Rock – Jazz classes
- Drama – Let it Be – Theatre Group – School
- Aerobics and Keep Fit Classes
- Windsurfing
- Librarian
- Badminton Club?
- Debating Society?
- Vegetarian Society?
- Member of Compassion in World Farming
- Volunteer work?
- Work for Father and various shops
- Work experience.

Monday 16th January 1984

Today I caught the bus and because I had not hardly worked during the weekend I had to take piles of work to school. School was v. boring indeed and when I got home at 4.30 p.m. I exercised and then I had a shower and washed my hair. I then went to drop off Charlotte's present (Birthday) and then went to Young Enterprise til 8.30 p.m. I got home and watched The Thornbirds but missed the most exciting bit (the Love Affair). Then Tez phoned me and told me that Danny told him I wasn't a virgin and I went absolutely mad and didn't know whether to deny it or not. I did not phone Danny.

Tuesday 17th January 1984

Today I went to school at 11 o'clock as I was v. tired and wanted more sleep. I got in for History and then I went to the library. School was totally pissing me off and I felt really really ugly. Anyway, after double Maths I went to the station with Tim Ward and then went home. Did my Economics homework all night. Watched Dallas. Went to bed at 12 o'clock which is really late – am very tired. I am v. annoyed at Danny and he hasn't phoned and I can't get it off my mind – the fuckin' bastard.

Wednesday 18th January 1984

Today I had a really horrible and boring morning's lessons. I had a good chat with Zoe and Helen at dinner though. We had Discourse in the afternoon but I wasn't in the mood and did not enjoy it as much as last week. I got the 3.20 p.m. train and got a taxi home. When I got home I did a bit of work and then exercised outside (twenty minutes) on bike (10 minutes) and dancing (10 minutes). Then I had a shower and washed my hair and watched Whicker's World. Wrote Sam's letter and then went to bed at 12 o'clock which is too late.

Thursday 19th January 1984

Today it was really cold and I felt a total wreck. I have got a really sore spot on my cheek which is really annoying me. Recently I have been getting really friendly with Helen and I really like her a lot. Today, I heard Denise Tang, Sammy Chadwick and Kate Elies bitching about me and I told Zoe Roberts and Kathryn Lewis of which one of them told Sammy who came up to me and felt a real prude. Anyway got home and tried to work but failed. Watched T.O.T.P and then David Attenborough and then the News and then a film about Finishing School and then a bit of Question Time. Went to bed at 11.30 and I was supposed to phone Tez but did not. I don't really want to go out this weekend.

Friday 20th January 1984

Today, I got the Coach, well just about by a split second, and I did my history notes in my free lessons. It seems to me that Stuart Hawkwood is sending rumours about him and me to spite me and to make everybody hate me as I grow more strong – the fuckin' bastard. I really hate him. Had a double History and then I went home. Next I watched TV, ate and had dinner. Then Jenny Mesri phoned me and said Max thought I was nice and we had a good chat. 1 must phone her. Then like a fool I watched TV until 1.30 and stuffed my face like a fat slob. I am going on a mainly fluid diet tomorrow.

Saturday 21st January 1984

Today I did nothing at all. I got up at 11.30 a.m. and watched TV, then I did a bit of History and watched TV, then I did a bit more History and talked to Terence. Then Helen phoned me and asked me to the Queensgate. Said no, went for a walk (twenty minutes). Watched TV and went to bed at 12.45 p.m. – very late.

Sunday 22nd January 1984

Today I woke up at 11.40 a.m. and had breakfast. I then did my history essay til 4 o'clock with restless breaks in between. Then I did some European History but have not learned anything yet. Have got to do my Economics. Watched The Thombirds. Washed hair, had shower. Did some more History and went to bed at 11.30 p.m. Up to today I have been taking my <u>vitamins</u> for 30 days.

Monday 23rd January 1984

Today I got the call at 8.20 a.m. and Daddy took me there. In the afternoon we had a test essay with Mrs Freer (History) and I did really terrible as per usual. It was awful weather today with snow and snow blizzards. I got home and watched TV. Did some Pure Maths and some History, didn't do any Economics and I have a test. Charlotte phoned me. I went to bed at 11.30 p.m. Missed my day of Multi Vitamins taking.

Tuesday 24th January 1984

Started Brewer's Yeast. Today I got the coach and I had double History, Oxbridge and then double History. Sue told Freer – to give up and I got left behind as Sue did all the talking – felt terrible must talk to Freer by myself. Anyway felt awful today and went to library for a bit and then home. Told Helen how I felt about everybody pissin' me off! And bitchy about me – Sue said nothing at all. Went home after Maths in which Andy said I was horrible lookin' – upset me a great deal. Got some sweets in Julliette. Got home, did some Economics, a bit of History and watched Dallas, went to bed at 11 o'clock – q good!

Wednesday 25th January 1984

Today the coach was extremely late and we got to school by 9.10 a.m. and I was late for my Economics' test which was first lesson. Then I had Stats and two more lessons. After lunch I went home at 1.30 p.m. as I did not want to do games. I watched TV plus did a bit of maths and I ate quite a lot. I hardly did the amount of work which I wanted to. Tez phoned me at last and we had quite a good chat. Then I watched TV for the rest of the night. Went to bed at 11.30 p.m. which is quite late.

Thursday 26th January 1984

Today, I got the coach and for once it was early. I had double Maths and Instats, we had a test in which I threw 8 marks down the drain through sheer carelessness. I was totally depressed after that. Did not have lunch, went to Careers Interview at 1.30 p.m. Lasted for one hour and was quite beneficial with a nice man. Got the 2.30 p.m. train and Mum picked me up. Went home and slobbed about and ate. Did a tiny bit of History but not a lot. Watched T.O.T.P and Living Planet. At 10.40 p.m. I did some exercises as I am getting so fat, for thirty minutes – then went to bed.

Friday 27th January 1984 Off School

Today, I did not go to school as I did not do my history essay in time to hand in for today, so I took the day off. I got up and tried to do my history and failed, so I washed my hair and showered and got ready to go to town. I went with Mum and ended up getting absolutely nothing, it was an awful waste of time (when I could have been working). I went to the Queensgate with Helen at 9.00 p.m. We had a good chat and decided to be close friends. Hooray! I really like her a lot. I felt a real mess tonight, my eyes watering everywhere etc. but

I felt really happy with her and hope she did with me. We took Helen and Lynne B. and Karen home.

Saturday 28th January 1984

Today, 1 went to School (Cheadle Hulme) to help with the Entrance Examination (8 years old). three girls got friendly with me and 1 liked Lucy (red) Sally (brown). Then got lift to station with Cath Hind. Went home, watched TV. Talked to Tez and got a Taxi to his house £12. Tez paid £5 everybody was there. It was Rob Hiton's last night before he went to Israel. Sarah and Kate and Simon were there. Afterwards at 12 o'clock went back to Danny's house and ate and had good fun. Left about 1 o'clock. Boy do I fancy Danny. Jim gave me a lift all the way home.

Sunday 29th January 1984

Today I woke up at 12 o'clock. Really tired, I had breakfast and started doing some work at 1.30 p.m. I worked from here until 4.30 p.m. and then I got ready to go to Mike Leon's house for a Jewish Meeting at 6. I phoned Jenny before this. I got to Didsbury and we discussed the Disco on the 25th February. Then I went back to Jenny's house till 9 o'clock. Spoke to Lucy and then home and went to bed at 11.15 p.m. which is very late seeing as I have been v. tired.

Monday 30th January 1984

Today, I had an okay day at school, I got back a history essay which I got 17 out of 25 for which I was not pleased about. Then I got home and did a bit of History. Then I had a shower and washed my hair and went to Parent's Evening at my school. It is a new system that kids are allowed to go to the evening with their parents to hear them moan about them. Miss McFadden = good, everything all right, I insulted her by saying went too fast and too many distractions. Mr Jones = thinks I worry, good up in the Huglin Thomas lot?! Persistent, or not much to say. Mrs Freer = wasn't there but I am quite encouraging (essays plain but effective and need polishing up Miss P). Mr Scaye = encouraging or should write essays quicker. Mr Chapman = right attitude, positive everything all right.

Tuesday 31st January 1984

Today, I did Oxbridge all by myself as Sue has given up. I did an Oxb. essay in a free for thirty minutes which is very good for me. I handed it in. Mrs Freer is away so we missed her history lesson. Had Maths (in recess stayed in Library with Helen) and got back a Stats test which was amazing 23/30. Then went home and did some History note making. Then I did some watching of Dallas and Alan Smith and Jones. Then did some Jane Fonda exercises (went a fifteen-minute walk with Dad) and had a shower and went to bed at 11.30 p.m. Read "My Cousin Rachael".

Chapter 2

February 1984

Wednesday 1st February 1984

Today got coach. Went to assembly. Had Maths, Economics, Maths (Pure) and then I went to the library until lunchtime. After lunch I went to Discocise which was okay but v. tiring. Then at 2.30 p.m. went to see a film (1 hour) on Universities in S14 by (Careers Advisor – Mr Wetton). Got the 10 to 4 train. Mum picked me up and we went to Wilmslow Leisure Centre to see how busy the swimming was. Saw Kate, Sammy and friend there (Sam had big boobs!) Didn't stay, went home did some work. Watched TV and exercised ten minutes on bike. Went to bed 11.36 p.m.

Thursday 2nd February 1984

Today missed the bus by two minutes and Martin had to take me to school. Had a double free and I helped in the library. Then I had a double Maths. Left school about 12.30 p.m. and I got the 1.20 train. Went to the Leisure Centre and swam from approx. 2 15 – 4.20 p.m. and breaks. Dad picked me up. I enjoyed the swimming (there were lots of fit buys there, working on their swimming). Went home. Charlotte phoned me and I watched T.O.T.P Went to bed at 11.40 p.m.

Friday 3rd February 1984

Today went to school with Julliette; did some library work. Then had Maths (Pure) and then actually went to the common room for a chat with people – quite enjoyed it. Then I had one lesson of History and then I went home (gave Will Rosen a lift home – creep). Got home, slopped about (went to Knutsford to try and look for a present for Sarah – failed). Phoned Danny, he was out. Tez phoned me and had a serious chat. I must phone Jenny M. Playing tennis tomorrow, walking with Lynne Bottomley. Phoned Lynne and we had a good chat. *Oxybet Tablets today*

Saturday 4th February 1984

Today 1 got up at 9 o'clock, washed hair and shower. Went to Alderley Edge Tennis Club. Met Lynne. Played for one hour. Walking 12 – 12.30 p.m. with David Potter – son (I was total shit with him and felt embarrassed). Went home. Phoned Danny and Helen. Then puked up. Helen went to Jaspers Wine Bar which was really nice. Had hummus, vegetable moussaka (Dutch), apple pie with cream. It was absolutely delicious and I really enjoyed myself.

Sunday 5th February 1984

Today I woke up at 12.00 p.m. I had some breakfast and then did a bit of History homework, but not enough to get on top of my work. I then went on my bike to the Wilmslow Tennis Club at 4.20 p.m. to see if there was a good wall to practice my tennis on. There was a wall but it was not very good. Then I had a shower and washed my hair. Then I had dinner and went to bed at 11 p.m. It was Sarah W's birthday today.

Monday 6th February 1984

Today I just about got the coach and I felt really depressed today because I had four spots on my face. Stayed in the library most of the day, went down to lunch with Joe and Helen. Then after afternoon lessons we walked to the station with Julliette and Tim. Then went to Wilmslow with Mum. Got Sarah a beautiful present £4.05 and went to Boots and WH Smith. Saw Vicki Pike and Ric Goddard. Got home and tidied my bedroom and did some homework. Had a big dinner, then phoned Charlotte for over an hour. Went to bed at 11.10 p.m.

Tuesday 7th February 1984

Today I missed the coach and Martin had to take me to school. I had double Oxbridge History which was terribly boring. Then double A-Level History – Mrs Freer came back. Then I had dinner and I didn't do any work really in the library. Oh, I gave Sarah's present today as well. Then I went home on the 3.20 train. I got a free Tennis Court from 5 – 6 p.m. I practiced against the wall and then from 5.40 until 6.10 p.m. Martin played with me for £3. Then from 6.10 – 6.50 p.m. I practiced against the wall. Went home, had a shower and washed my hair. Charlotte came to see me at 8.20 p.m. left after ten minutes (v vain girl). Then watched Dallas and did some work (got to bed at 10.30 p.m.!!!!)

Wednesday 8th February 1984

Today I got the coach as I got up earlier at 7.00 a.m. exactly. Had four lessons. Then went to lunch with Helen and Rooky. I then had Discocise which was extremely boring and caught the 3.20 train. Went home did some History, went on a walk with Mum to Yew Tree. Stuffed myself with food. Must diet for Saturday. David Patterson phoned to give me a time for coaching on Saturday. Watched TV. Stuffed myself with food. Realised that I had lost the calculator and felt sick to the bone; I must find it. Went to bed at 10.40 p.m.

Thursday 9th February 1984

Today it was freezing cold and I had double duties for the exams. I went through the day with Helen and I got friendly with Stuart once again who is usually nice or terrible to me. I got home and did homework and then I went on a walk with Mum and we went to Yew Tree. Watched T.O.T.P and Gary was on it. I then watched a bit of David Attenborough. I then phoned Jenny Hesru who kept me talking until 9 o'clock and I did not have time to wash my hair. She invited me to London next week. I phoned Lynne. I went to bed at 11.30 p.m. which is late.

Stuart starts being nice

Friday 10th February 1984

Today I went to school later because I was tired. I woke up at 8 o'clock. I got to school by 10.40 a.m. I tried to see Mr Buckley but failed. It was an awful day today, Maths/Double History. I have got a lot of work to do this weekend and do not know how I am going to fit it all in. I got home and did a bit of work. Lucy phoned me about the Jewish weekend in London and tried to persuade me to go without success. Stuart phoned me to make friends and he fancies me and wants to go out with me. Then Tez phoned me and I brushed him off as usual. I did twenty minutes of walking outside and then I did ten minutes on the bike.

Saturday 11th February 1984

Today I got up and had tennis coaching at Alderley from 11.30 – 12.30 p.m. and my backhand was really awful and I was totally embarrassed. Then I played with Lynne from 1.45 to 3.15 p.m. and it was okay. Got home. Danny phoned; Jenny phoned. I phoned Helen and Tez. Stayed in and got to bed at 12.10 p.m. On a diet from tomorrow onwards.

Forty-five mins

Sunday 12th February 1984

Today, tried to do some work but could not. Jim phoned me to see if I could go out but couldn't. Walked for twenty-five minutes. Had a shower and washed my hair. Went to Ric's house for Shekels meeting with Jenny. Got back home at 10.30 p.m. and went to bed at 11.11 p.m., v. late.

Monday 13th February 1984

Today, I had a horrible day at school. I had piles of work to do and still have. I got home and tried to do, or rewrite my history essay which I had done yesterday. I found it came a bit easier to me as I tried to use my own words but it still needs a lot more work which I must do. I got ready for Young Enterprise and Stuart Hawkswood picked me up and took me there. I got elected as managing director and I tried to organise the company with the help of Ian Wetherall and James Pink. Got home about 9.15 p.m. Had tea. Did some more History essay. Then got to bed at 11.20 p.m. which is quite late. No exercise today.

Got a Valentines Card from Stuart. Ah!

Tuesday 14th February 1984

Today I was totally shattered and 1 felt awful at school. I had a lot to eat today, lots of chocolate caramel shortbread made by the Domestic Science people i.e. Helen, and I nicked some Neapolitans, five to be exact, from a bag in the cloakroom. I did not have any lunch. I got home finished off my essay. I watched TV. Tez called me and he had failed his test, I was annoyed and I don't know why. There's a party tomorrow at "Thursdays" (Rose Askanazi, Jackie Barratt) and I'm probably going to it. I don't know. Had a shower tonight. Went to bed at 12.16 a.m. which is very late.

Wednesday 15th February 1984

Today 1 did not go to school as I was too tired. I missed four lessons today. I got up late and got ready for town late. I got the train to town at 3.05 p.m. and I got in town at 4 o'clock. Miss Selfridge had a lot of nice clothes but I did not know what to get. Anyway, looked in most shops and I didn't know what to buy and all I got was a hypoallergenic foundation and some things from Boots. I regretted going to Manchester at all because I was very tired when I got back. Tez, Jenny and Jim all phoned me. Tez and me finished. Hooray!! I would have gone to an ace Jewish party where everybody was going, at "Thursdays" in town, but did not. Bed at 11.45 p.m.!

Off School. A Valentine from Tez

Thursday 16th February 1984

Today it was my last day at school and I had horrible double Maths today. I had an okay day but also a very busy day. After school went to town and bought a pair of dungarees (£27) for weekend in London. I also got some makeup. I got home at 7 o'clock and Jenny phoned me. Watched TV and I went to bed at 11.40 p.m. which is very late.

My period started today.

Friday 17th February 1984

Today I got up about 9 a.m. and went to Wilmslow at 11 o'clock. Looked around and bought a pair of Second Image Jeans (£18) and a pink jumper from Benetton (£30) I then got home at 10 o'clock, I got ready to go on this Jewish weekend in London. I was twenty minutes late at Jen's house. Got to Manchester Piccadilly and got the 4.11 train. There was a delay on the train and we arrived from tube and bus at YMCA about 9.30 p.m. (the train journey was fun) Had dinner and got to know a few people and had five programmes until 1.30 p.m. Went to Johnny Morris's house. Did not get to bed till 3 o'clock and then I couldn't sleep on a crap bed. It was a fun start to the weekend and quite a few boys fancied me.

Went to bed at 3 am and washed hair (W.H.)

Saturday 18th February 1984

Today, got up and found out that Fraser and Johnny Morris fancied me. Johnny Morris was gorgeous *{Diagram of Johnny's Face}* black hair, really fit body, gorgeous face. He flirted with me a lot etc. throughout the day. I felt really tired all day. I managed to get to my room in-between programmes (to rest and re-do makeup). At night stayed with Johnny all the time. We sang songs and talked it was really great. Stayed up until 4.30 a.m. with Johnny it was really good. I really really like him.

W.H. No Tennis

Sunday 19th February 1984

Today got up at 8 o'clock. Went down for breakfast at 9. Stayed with Johnny all day. At 2 o'clock went from the YMCA and went to Euston Station with Johnny. Said goodbye and was really sad. On the train it was good fun. Sat with Stuart Merks and Ed Viner. Talked to others and Johnny Chestock was really horrible to me and he said I had a complex. Got off at Stockport with Mark Hanburger and Sarah Cotton and Ed; went to Wilmslow. Got home and then went to Hallal with Ayan and Fatiyana May. Got to bed at 2 o'clock. Very tired indeed.

W.H.

Monday 20th February 1984

Today I woke up at 12 o'clock, Had a very big breakfast. Listened to the radio. Spoke to Helen on the phone as she had phoned me and I told her I wanted to go to The Valley Lodge on Tuesday 21st and stay the night at her house. Okay. Then watched TV and would you believe it Tez phoned me. Did not speak though because I wanted to watch ice skating. Got ready for YE. And was my first time at the Head as the Managing Director. Richard (Advisor) said that I was good and that I organised it well. I was happy and enjoyed it probably for the first time. Went to bed at 12.45 a.m. after TV. Felt lonely today as I missed all my friends on the London trip, especially Johnny – (I like him a lot).

I love Johnny and want to be less lonely.

Tuesday 21st February 1984

Today I got up about 11 o'clock and had breakfast. Ric Michael phoned me and then I tried to do some homework but failed. Zoe phoned me up. Asked me to see a video and I accepted. I watched the British Rock and Pop Awards and Dallas and then went to Helen's house where Kay Watson was. We went to The Valley Lodge it was okay apart from being hot and I had no money for drinks and felt a total mess and I hate those places. Left at 1 o'clock and got to bed at 3 a.m. Helen and I talked. I stayed the night and we had cheese sandwiches and hot milk, Washed Hair (W.H.).

Wednesday 22nd February 1984

Today I wanted to play tennis with Lynne but it was called off. This morning I woke up at Helen's and felt absolutely awful and wheezy. She gave me some breakfast and Mum picked me up at 12 o'clock. In the afternoon I tidied my bedroom and got organised. I phoned Zoe and I phoned Charlotte. I phoned Lynne and Julliette. I phoned Bunny to get a lift back from Zoe's. Stuart phoned me. We had a good chat. Jenny also phoned me today and I forgot to phone her back. Bed at 11.50 p.m.

Thursday 23rd February 1984

Today I got up at 9 a.m. and washed my hair. I played Tennis with Lynne at Alderley at 1.30 – 3.30 p.m. as she could not play at 11.30 a.m.. I did some History beforehand, then went to see Mill Street Cottages with Mum and Dad and Chelsea Pine Shop (which is being made into a house to let). Then got home and phoned Jenny who told me two nasty rumours (about Tez and Johnny) both not true, I was pissed off. I got ready for Zoe's dinner party. Got to Bramhall at 9 o'clock and watched "Private Lessons" and ate a lot of food. Then got home at 12.10 a.m. and went to bed at 12.30 a.m. which is extremely late.

Friday 24th February 1984

Today I got up at 9.45 a.m., had breakfast and tried to do some work. I went to see Dr August in Knutsford and he spoke to Mum on her own most of the time. Then got home and ready for meeting at Didsbury. Got the pizzas from Hale Bams (£21) and then went to Didsbury by 2.45 p.m. (should have got there at 2 p.m.) and put them out then the band Catch 22 came and practiced a little. Then Mum took me to Altrincham where I bought a bag, belt and white jumpsuit (£30) from Pink Cadillac. The doc gave me some hormone tablets, then got home; spoke to Tez (broke friends), Jim Salem and that's it. Went to bed at 11.40 p.m.

Saturday 25th February 1984

Had tennis lesson from 10 – 10.45 a.m. (45 mins) but I was ten minutes late. Got home and felt totally depressed. Stuart Hawkwood phoned and Sam. Got ready for Disco; wore a white jumpsuit. Had three spots on my face. Johnny Lewis was there and he is extremely fit, but he doesn't fancy me anymore. It was a rubbish disco and Luch shouted at me for not tidying up at the end. But I couldn't as I had a lift waiting for me. Got home about 1 o'clock. Bed at 2 o'clock.

Sunday 26th February 1984

Got up at 11 o'clock. Started History essay at 2 o'clock and worked until 3 o'clock. Phoned Sarah and Ed and picked them up at 6.45 p.m. Got to Menorah at 7.10 p.m. and had quite a good time except that Stuart and Johnny weren't being that nice to me, probably because I looked shattered. I felt awful. Jenny came. Got home by Ed Viner's dad at 10 p.m. Watched an Australian film – "My Brilliant Career" – good. Got to bed at 1 o'clock. Not going to school tomorrow.

Monday 27th February 1984

Today I had another day off school, my third day off this term. I got up at 11.30 a.m. and I started working at 1 p.m. All I did today was to finish my History and English essay. I got to bed at 11.30 p.m. and I have to wake up at 7 a.m. tomorrow. I phoned Sarah and we spoke for an hour. I told her about all the rumours going around about me and she told me to laugh at them. (Okay.) Charlotte phoned me. I really don't want Sam to go back to Devon. Sam came down last Wednesday.

Tuesday 28th February 1984

Today I managed to get to school though I missed the bus. I felt really shattered. Anyway, I went through the day and it was like hell. Left School at 3 p.m. and got home about 4 p.m. Phoned Sam at Louise's house and then I met her at the Plough at 8 p.m. She looked really nice with longer hair. Stuart, Louise and Chris (her boy) were there. Sad when Sam left. Today I have eaten so bloody much. Tomorrow I am on diet. Bed 11.44 p.m.

Wednesday 29th February 1984

Today I had an awful day at school – it was dead boring. I had Discocise and I really tried to work hard. Got home about 4.45 p.m. Ate some food (as usual) Did some work (History). Then did some exercises for thirty-five minutes because I felt so fuckin' fat. I am 9 stone now and I should be 8 stone so I must diet from now on. Then Charlotte phoned me and I then had a shower and some more food and got to bed at 11.40 p.m. Late as per usual. Dave Patterson phoned to change tennis time.

Chapter 3

March 1984

Thursday 1st March 1984

Today I got to school and went straight to the library to revise for my Maths test as I had forgotten my file last night. I revised Pure Maths and did okay in the test. Then I went to the library and did some work. Today John Yates said my legs were nice. Of course, and his friend said they were nice yesterday. After school I met Lynne in Alderley and we played tennis from 4.20 – 5.00 p.m. and then I practiced my serves from 5 – 5.30 p.m. Then I went home, binged as per usual and then watched T.O.T.P and ate a lot and then I did some work from 9.15 – 11 p.m. I went to bed at 11.30 p.m. as well!!! Which is late. Today, Dad told me some good news; I am going to Spain on 12th – 26th April.

Friday 2nd March 1984

Today had an okay day at school, except that it was very windy plus v. cold. I got through the day wondering whether Julliette and I were going to play tennis. We decided not to as it was too windy. Got home and went with Mum to Wilmslow Leisure Centre. On the Solarium an hour – £1.50, and then I swam which I did not enjoy because there were too many people and I did not exercise enough. Had dinner and stuffed myself til I got to bed at 11.45 p.m. The house was absolutely freezing today as well.

Started Diane (for my skin – it's supposed to clear up acne).

Saturday 3rd March 1984

Got up at 9.30 a.m. – washed hair and showered. Went to Tennis at 12 – 1 p.m. (1 hour) With David (cor!) and saw Joe who saw Dave. Frances Payne saw me plus her friend? coaching – oh dear. Phoned Lynne played from 2–3.30 p.m. 6-4 (the tennis game). Lynne had a good game. Next I did not get picked up until 7.30 p.m., annoyed and angry with my mum. Watched TV until 11.50 p.m. and then went to bed.

Sunday 4th March 1984

Got up at 11.45 a.m., had breakfast and listened to Piccadilly Top 40. Watched TV and slobbed about. Sarah Cotton phoned about going out. I decided I was not going. Stuart Michaels phoned about my speech. Did an Economics essay, had shower and washed hair. Went to bed at 11.30 p.m. Ate too much today.

Monday 5th March 1984

Today I went to school with three spots on my face and a terrible red big sore spot on the side of my nose. I studied Oxbridge. Mr Scaye and Mrs Freer wondered if I was trying to tell them if I was giving up. Oh dear. Decided to give up anyhow. Next I had six lessons today. Fuck! Ate a few sweets and then went home. Ate bread, biscuits (2), oat cakes, fruit, carocottes, etc. Went to Y.E. it was a real shambles and came home and ate a great deal more. Stuart phoned and I said I would phone him back tomorrow. Bed at 11.20 p.m.!

Tuesday 6th March 1984

Today I gave up Oxbridge and I had double History and I had double Maths. I felt awful today because I had two great big spots on my face. One on my nose which I squeezed at school and one on the side of my lip as per usual. I got home, binged, washed hair and had shower. Watched Dallas, spoke to Stuart from 9.45–11.10 p.m., phew! Made me go to bed late, got to bed at 12.30 a.m., the latest yet! Squeezed two spots. Also went on sunbed today. 4 hours = £1.50.

Dad and Martin go to India

Wednesday 7th March 1984

Today I went to school and had four boring lessons. I had a really big break. At lunchtime I did some work and had to see Discocise teacher to excuse myself as I forgot my letters. Went home with a Taxi at 3 o'clock. Rested until 5 p.m. and then worked until 7.20 p.m. Had dinner watched Coronation Street. Then watched Brookside and Fame. I binged myself after dinner a bit. Spoke to Tez on the phone and then Jenny until 10 o'clock. Then had piles of bloody cheddar cheese (so fattening). On a binge of course. Went to bed after doing more History at 11.30 p.m.

Thursday 8th March 1984

Today I did not feel like going to school. But I had to go and it was a v. boring day. Had double Maths and double Economics. I had a very dry spot on my cheek where a spot had been yuk! After school we went to Gilberts and to Side Kicks where I tried a white track suit for £18 which was quite nice. I think I am going to get it if it is still there. Hopefully it will be. Then got home and need to do my essay. I finished it tonight thank God. Watched T.O.T.P. and then forty minutes exercise but spoiled it by having three oatcakes and two tangerines, apples, etc. Went to bed at 11.30 p.m. Very late as per usual.

Friday 9th March 1984

Today 1 had to do my history essay at school. I was in a bad mood all day as a new spot came on my face. I had a shower and washed my hair this morning before school! I then had a bad day at school. I played tennis with Julliette but it was hopeless, I was playing crap and she is not as good as me! Mum picked me up at 5.30 p.m. and she had bought my white tracksuit from Side Kicks for £18. We went home and then went to Solarium at 7.15 p.m. Saw three hunks who look after the swimming pool. Yum! Watched TV. I went to bed at 1 o'clock which is very late.

Saturday 10th March 1984

Today washed hair, had coaching lesson at 2.30 p.m. (an hour) where I played lousy, really lousy. Had quite a revealing chat with David who I madly fancy. Watched TV and before that I went to Side Kicks, bought a top (cool) £10. Went to

Danielle Hymans at 9 p.m. Went to The Sandpiper – ate a lot of junk and drink. Good time. Danielle and Gill – really nice. I fancy Andrew Kingsley – Cor!

Sunday 11th March 1984

Today I got up at 11 a.m. and had breakfast. I was trying to slim today and I was quite successful apart from a few binges of bread. I went for a walk today with Mum. Phoned Charlotte. Stuart M phoned and I said I would not be going to the same event in March. He was mad with me. Did a bit of homework, some exercises and went to bed at 11.10 p.m. I don't feel like going to school tomorrow.

Monday 12th March 1984

Today went to school although I did not feel like it at all. I saved Oxbridge and Helen is being funny towards me going off with Rooky (prob, from the hols ha ha!) In History Mrs Freer shouted at me viciously, so I defended myself against her. The bitch. When I got home I ate a lot. Got ready to go to The Palace from Cheadle Hulme. I got the coach, stayed with Tracy, Liza and Gwenda. Saw West Side Story – very good but a bit boring. All the same – I enjoyed myself eating sweets and Maltesers. Got home and stuffed myself with anything I could get my hands on. Went to bed at 12 o'clock.

Tuesday 13th March 1984

Today, I officially gave up Oxbridge as I was sent for by Miss Pilkington (she hates me though). Had double History and double Maths. Helen is going off with Rooky still and she is not going to Metbelle – hooray! Mum went to hospital to have a lump taken out of her shoulder and she came back and is all right. I did a bit of History and a bit of exercise. Washed hair, watched Dallas, ate and then watched a fantastic Film called "The Castle Ball". Bed 11.30 p.m.

Wednesday 14th March 1984

Today I went to school not feeling very well and I went through the lessons feeling ill but did not want to miss them. However, Mum said she would pick me up at 12.30 p.m. but did not come until 1.20 p.m. Went home, watched TV, ate and then went to bed at 4 until 7.30 p.m., then phoned Sarah and Julliette. Felt rather ill so went to bed at 10 o'clock and fell asleep. Woke up at 4.35 a.m. to go to toilet. Felt really ill.

Thursday 15th March 1984

Today I had the day off school as I had a bad cough and cold. I went to bed all day and tried to get some sleep. I had diarrhoea later on which made me feel absolutely awful. I went to Cheadle Hulme School (C.H.S.) Career Convention because I thought I would be missing a good opportunity. I really should not have gone as I felt totally ill. Went to a law talk and then to a law person (Higginbottom) who talked about law. I got home at 9 o'clock and had something to eat. Went to bed at 11 o'clock.

Friday 16th March 1984

Today I had the day off school again and stayed in bed most of the day trying to get better. Mum went out and got me some cough sweets. I had four phone calls today, from Charlotte, Stuart Hawkwood, Helen and Stuart Marks. I watched TV with Mum and we had dinner. I phoned David P. to tell him I won't make my tennis lesson. Went to bed at about 11 o'clock. Dad phoned from India today and I spoke to him.

Saturday 17th March 1984

Today it was quite cold and I was quite glad I was not playing tennis. I did a bit of History and Economics. I phoned Helen and I had a big lunch, lots of cheese. Then I watched Joan Rivers on TV and it was excellent. Went to bed at 11.40 p.m.

No walking

Sunday 18th March 1984

Today, got up at 10 a.m., had breakfast (a big one). I did my Economics essay at 12–3 o'clock. Then had a break and washed my hair and had a bath. Then watched Dynasty with my big dinner, which was a big bowl of spaghetti and pesto sauce, yum! I went to bed at 10.30 p.m., realised today must go to bed at least by 10 o'clock.

Monday 19th March 1984

Today I went to school with a really big spot on my chin. It was a dobber and very sore. My hair also was a total mess as usual. I have got a horrible History essay to do for Mr Scaife. Went through the day. Did a bit of History but after that just ate dinner and a whole more after dinner and Stuart Marks phoned me and also I read Guardian and went to bed at 11 o'clock.

Tuesday 20th March 1984

Today had an awful day at school. Got home with Granny and ate quite a bit of snacks and History essay from 4.30 til 7 p.m. Squeezed spot but that did not go much better. Had dinner with Dallas. Ate a great deal. 3 slices of bread, piles of lentils plus salad and mayonnaise and pear and apple and some cheese (cheddar). I absolutely stuffed myself because of my history essay and took out quite a big amount of hair from my head by twiddling my hair. Depressed. Nearly finished essay. Bed at 12 a.m.!

Wednesday 21st March 1984

Today I was very tired and did not feel like four lessons all in the morning. However, I got through them all right and went to the tuck shop with Rachel H. at break. Had dinner and then had Discourse which I quite enjoyed. Got home by 3.30 p.m. and caught the 2.50 Train. Ate some food – 250 cals to 300 cals. Did History essay. Went for a walk at 6.50 to 7.15 p.m., then had dinner at 8 p.m. while watching Fame. Lynne phoned. Decided to play tennis, also David P phoned – had a good chat and worked out a time for tennis. Watched "The Other Half" on TV. Very interesting about Playboy and Bunny Girl. Went to bed at 10.30 p.m., after big meal, ate about 350 calorie binge!

Thursday 22nd March 1984

Today I went to school as per usual and had Maths and double Economics. Went on train to Alderley and met Lynne who played tennis with me from 4.30 til 5.30/45 p.m. We just were getting warmed up and Mum came to pick me up. I got home and had a shower, washed my hair. Then I had dinner while watching T.O.T.P. and then I did some work. At about 11 p.m. I had a binge of about 600 calories. Went to bed at 12 o'clock. Did Dave Melus's homework.

Finished Diane

Friday 23rd March 1984

Today I got up at 7.30 a.m. and had a big breakfast. Went to School late as I had to do some Pure Maths homework. Had dinner then went to play tennis with Julliette. Ate sweets, apple and bun beforehand. We played outside for about half an hour but it was very cold. Got back and ate then went to Safeway. Got home, had dinner, phoned Stuart Marks and then I ate piles of fruit after my meal. Must eat less from now on. Next I went to bed at 11.10 p.m.

Started Diane

Saturday 24th March 1984

Today got up at 10 a.m. Had breakfast, washed hair and went to coaching lesson with David for half an hour from 11.45 til 12.30 p.m. It was not cold. After I went home and had a binge from 12–4 o'clock. I did not want to do any work. Went to "Thursdays" tonight with Stuart M, Paul L, Caroline Shapiro, saw Anthony Adker, Tez, Johnny Lewis, all looked fit. Felt a mess. Did not get to bed until 3 o'clock.

Stuart took me home and Jerusalem rings. Cycled and skipped
45 minutes.

Sunday 25th March 1984

Today, I got up at 12 o'clock. Had my breakfast. Then I worked from 1 until 7 o'clock doing my history notes. Had diarrhoea. Washed hair. Watched Dynasty while eating dinner. Today I did not have a binge. I felt really good. Went to bed late though at 11.30 p.m. Cheryl cancelled tennis. *Skipped and cycled.*

Monday 26th March 1984

Today I woke up extremely tired. At school I had to revise for my Economics test which I did really rubbish in. So there. Then I had double History and Economics which was profusely boring. Got home and ate and had tea. Relaxed until 5 p.m. Worked from 5 til 6.30 p.m. on History Europe notes for essay. Went to Y.E. at 7 til 8.30 p.m. Extremely boring and not enjoying it. Sarah and Stuart also there. Came home, had dinner and quite a big pudding i.e. dates, fruit, prunes, jam Ryvita etc. Did some more work. Bed 11.20 p.m.

Exercise bike – 10 minutes

Tuesday 27th March 1984

Today I went to school feeling depressed as I was thinking about my History Europe essay. When I got back home from school I ate quite a lot (500 calories) including tahini, fruit and prunes. I then did my essay from 7.55 p.m. I watched Dallas with a big dinner (so depressed) and a big binge after (cottage cheese, fruit, bread and butter etc.). Jenny and Charlotte phoned. Had shower, washed hair. Did work from 10 – 11.30 p.m. and then finished. Ate a little. Went to bed at 11.20 p.m.

Wednesday 28th March 1984

Today went to school with Mum so I could get up later. Had lessons then had Discocise. Came home and ate about 400 calories. Went to sun bed. Phoned Cheryl, Lynne and Danny, Charlotte and Jenny. Had a big dinner and a binge after it as well. All this added to a depressed me. Went to bed at 11.20 p.m.

Cycled on bike — twenty minutes

Thursday 29th March 1984

Today I went to school with Mum. Had lessons. After school had organised to play tennis with Lynne, but it was raining like mad and we did not bother. I went home, had my dinner about 7.30 p.m. At about 11 p.m. I had my only binge of about 400 calories. I don't know why but all I know is I won't do it again. Stuart M and Tom Moore phoned. Bed at 11.35 p.m.

Cycled and skipped – 30 minutes

Friday 30th March 1984

Today I went to school and had a triple free. At break I went with Stuart to sell the Y.C. jewellery. Sold £3.20 worth. Then I had Maths and got test back as well. I was in a rather bad mood today as everything was getting on top of me. Played tennis with Julliette and Lynne and Paula were playing on another court. Really good. Mum picked me up and we had to go to school as I forgot a book but it was really in Fran's room. My room being decorated at moment so I had to sleep in Mum's. Bed 12.05 a.m.

Saturday 31st March 1984

Today I got up at about 10 o'clock and had breakfast. Had shower and washed hair. Had coaching at 2.30 – 3 p.m. (An hour) which was really awful. Then went to Knutsford with Mum, then came home. I had an awful binge of 1000 calories, felt absolutely awful til 9.30 p.m. when I started exercising for one hour – cycling, skipping. Bed 12.05 a.m.

Chapter 4

April 1984

Sunday 1st April 1984

Today I got up at about 10 o'clock. Had breakfast and then I decided to do some work. I did some History, watched "Fiddler on the Roof". Jenny phoned me! Thought Daddy was coming back but he didn't. Watched Dynasty. Had a binge and went to bed at 12 o'clock. Slept in Mum's bed.

Cycled – 10 minutes

Monday 2nd April 1984

Today I decided to go to school later as I was very tired. Had shower and washed hair and then I did some History notes til 12.30 p.m. Mum gave me a lift to school. After school played tennis with Cheryl. She beat me 6 – 4. Lynne and Paula were playing on the other court. Lynne beat Paula 6-3. Got home. Went to Young Ethiopian (Y.E.) at 7 o'clock. Very boring. Then walked to Leisure Centre at 8 p.m. but did not go on sunbed (quite sunny today). Got home, had dinner, watched TV til 10 45 p.m. John from L.A. phoned me. I was very surprised. He wanted to see me like mad. I said I would write. Bed at 12 o'clock.

Tuesday 3rd April 1984

Today I went into school by the bus. I was in the library with David Hornsby and Gavin. Then I had double History and then I had double Maths. Played tennis with Paula which I really enjoyed. She beat me 6-3. Dad came back from India today with presents and I had a great big binge. Then I went to bed and at 10 o'clock I had diarrhoea for half an hour. Not too bad. Went to bed at 11.30 p.m. and decided not to go to school—too much on – Hooray!

Wednesday 4th April 1984

Today I had a day off school because I had to wash hair and shower. Also wanted to go to Beau Geste which closed at 2 p.m. and I did not want to do Discocise so I got ready to go to Beau Geste and arrived there at 12.30 and stayed until 2 p.m. I did not get an outfit for Tiffany's tonight so decided I did not want to go. Phoned Helen to tell her I was not going. Had quite a big binge. Watched Song for Europe – crap. Went to bed. Felt really awful.

Skipped

Thursday 5th April 1984

Today I went to school and apparently Tiffany's was quite good. I got through the day okay but when Dad and Mum went out I had quite a big binge and felt a right fuckin' pig. I went to bed about 1 o'clock. I did some History today also. Weather really nice today and Dad could not play tennis with me.

Friday 6th April 1984

Today I got up about 10 a.m. and had a very big breakfast. Worked from 11 til 3 o'clock doing European History notes and I still have piles more to do. Lynne phoned me and told me she did not want to play tennis. I was dead mad with her. Dad would not play tennis. Went to sunbed at 8.45 p.m. Got home, washed hair and showered. Had something to eat. Bed at 12.30 a.m. Tennis tomorrow.

Exercise bike — twenty minutes

Saturday 7th April 1984

Today I had my coaching lesson with David at 10 – 10.45 a.m. It was okay. Then got home and went back with Dad to play tennis at 3 o'clock and David was still there. After one hour of tennis (me and Dad) we went to Wilmslow i.e. Sainsbury's and Gilberts to get a demo racket. I got home and got ready to go to Wythenshawe Forum to see "Having a Ball". It was hilarious. I went with Jenny (and rest of crowd were there) and we went back to her house and we stayed until 12.20 a.m. Got taken home.

Sunday 8th April 1984

Today I got up very late, had breakfast and then I did something until tennis at 3 p.m. with Paula. I went on my bike and I lost with my demo racket 6-0. I was extremely annoyed. Got back and listened to Top 40 and then had shower and washed hair. Watched a film called "Patrick" – it was amazing.

Monday 9th April 1984

Today I got up quite early and had breakfast. Then Mum and I went to town. We went to lots of shops – In Wear, Boots, Warehouse, Midas, Miss Selfridge "Wear" etc. I did not get everything in the end. Anyway got home at 6.30 p.m. and had to go to Y.E. Got there and we decided to have another one unfortunately. Oh dear! Got home at 8.30 p.m., ate, hair, got ready to go to Tiffany's. Left at 10.20 p.m., arrived there at 11 p.m. It was quite good. Tez, Fraser, Stuart, Ed and Paul Lisberg were there and Gavin, David, Tim. It was Ric's and Ed Alexander's party. Got home at 2 a.m. Went to bed after 3 a.m. and I ate a bit when I got home.

Tuesday 10th April 1984

Today, it was raining and it was a horrible day I did a bit of History notes while Mum went shopping. It was the day before my birthday and Mum and Dad and I decided to go for dinner. Washed hair and had shower and then we watched Dallas. After Dallas we went out and I had a vegetable curry dish which was delicious. It was quite an enjoyable meal out.

Wednesday 11th April 1984

Today it was my birthday and I became 17-years-old. I got a card from Mum and Grandma (£5) and two cards in the post from Tim and Ric. I got ready to go to Wilmslow to get a few things. Stayed here until 4 o'clock, buying from B&D etc. White belt, boots and a lady shaver. Went home and received my present from Sarah W (a pair of pink socks). Came home and ate a lot!! Also then Ric phoned me, then finished my packing because I am going to Spain tomorrow. Organised my work for the holiday. Got to bed at 12 o'clock after piles of packing.

Thursday 12th April 1984

Today I got up at 6.50 a.m. and washed my hair. Then I got ready to go to Manchester Airport. We were extremely late and could not go shopping anywhere. We had to get on the plane immediately. Missed W H Smith etc and all the nice shops. Got on plane and arrived in Malaga at 1.45 p.m. (our time), 12.45 p.m. (Spain time). Got to our apartment and went on the beach; it was quite hot. Then unpacked and washed my hair. We then went to Ayrora (a little village on a hill, very near to us). I had 2 salads, (asparagus *I* mixed and bread and prunes) and salad cream. How many calories? Bed 12.07 a.m.

Exercised

Friday 13th April 1984

Today I got up and it was raining in Spain. The weather was awful. I had prunes for breakfast and coffee. At about 2 p.m. after doing some English History (approximately two hours). Had my dinner which was 300 calories but when Mum and Dad went out had a binge of bread, prunes, banana (800). I was very guilty and nuts after. Did some more work and I got ready for tennis with Dad at 3 until 6 p.m. which was excellent. Then we went to Ayrora for dinner. I had a salad and bread and fruit. Exercised for twenty-five minutes. Bed at 1 a.m

Awful

Saturday 14ᵗʰ April 1984

Today once again the weather was awful. Cloudy, rainy and cold. I had my breakfast and then did some work. After 3 o'clock Mum and I had lunch and then I read and we went for a walk along the Promenade – 4.30 until 5.30 p.m.. At 6 o'clock Dad and I played tennis and then Mum played. I beat her – 6-3. We then went to Benalmedena village for a lovely meal and came home and I had eight prunes! Very bad.

Exercised – thirty-five minutes
Awful

Sunday 15ᵗʰ April 1984

Today the weather was okay. It was a bit cloudy and windy but Mum and me could sunbathe for a while. I spoke to Pepé and Habille today. At 6 o'clock I played tennis with Dad until 7 p.m. We went to Tivoli tonight. It was okay. I went on three rides all by myself. We ate nut brittle, apples etc. and there were lots of shows. It is a good or brill amusement park. I exercised when I got home.

Awful

Monday 16ᵗʰ April 1984

Today it was a beautiful day with no clouds in the sky. We went down to the beach and sunbathed. Then we had lunch. I played tennis with Dad and was beating him 4-3 and 4-5. At 5.30 p.m. we went down to the beach and saw Paco (oh my God!). I went with him last year a couple times. After this I came up to the flat, washed hair and showered and ate quite a lot and we had our seder for; it was the first day of Pesach. We had quite a big meal and my tummy was absolutely bulging. 1 exercised for fifteen minutes and I went to bed at 10 o'clock very late.

Tuesday 17th April 1984

Today it started off quite horrible. Then it cleared up about 12 o'clock. Mum and I stayed on the beach most of the day and I played Tennis with Dad at 6–7 p.m.. He beat me 6-1 because I played quite horribly. Anyway after this we went to one of the restaurants on the beach which was quite nice. Did not do any exercise tonight.

Wednesday 18th April 1984

Today I got up early to go to Fuengirola but waited one hour for the bus and two passed by. They were completely full. Anyway went down to the beach. I saw Paco, Habille, Rafaelle, on the beach and spoke to Habille for an hour. Then in the afternoon after a binge of macaroons and cakes from the fridge, which I felt awful after, I walked with Paco, Habille and Rafaelle for the Spanish Tour of Bicycles for 1 1/4 hours watching all the fun. At 7–8 p.m. I played Habille at tennis, I beat him 6-1. He was crap. Then I went out with two Dutch girls and Paco, Habille and Rafaelle to a wine bar. We ate and drank and I got home at 1 o'clock. I really like Paco – Cor!

No exercise

Thursday 19th April 1984

Today Dad came back from being away. Paco was leaving today. I mostly stayed on the beach today. I did not play tennis during the day today, but when Dad returned from his cycling trip, we played from 7–8 p.m. Dad beat me of course. Dad and Mum went out and I stayed in totally depressed and ate a lot.

Friday 20th April 1984

Today there were no courts free and I could not play tennis. I got talking to the American boys at the swimming pool today and they are called John (I fancy him), Bill (really funny) and Steve (really nice – beard). They go to Lancaster University as part of their American course in Minnesota, America. John invited me to come over later on which I did for a while. At about 11 o'clock we went for a walk on the beach and it was fun. 1 got home at about 1 o'clock. (Henry comes and Dad and him go cycling tomorrow).

Saturday 21st April 1984

Today the weather was not too cool as it was very windy. I went for a jog with John and Bill but I had my period and it was awful and embarrassing. Then I played tennis 7–8 p.m. with Cecily and Margaret's (Dutch girl) father who is quite good. 1 beat him 5-3. I then went to John's for dinner which was delicious, really nicely made. I enjoyed myself a great deal; it was good fun. Got back at 1 o'clock.

Awful

Sunday 22nd April 1984

Today the weather was awful and I was totally depressed, I stayed with John a lot. I played Tennis with Bill at 3 – 4 p.m. He beat me 6-0 and John's new friend Steve came. Tonight we went to Benalmedena to a Dutch bar. It was Bill's last night. I walked home with John along the promenade.

Awful

Monday 23rd April 1984

Today it was another awful day and John, Steve and Steve all went to Grenada. In the morning I went for a walk and afternoon time I went to Fuengirola with Mum and we bought a black bikini. We came back and saw John and Steve playing hacky sack. I didn't play tennis today. I went to see John, Steve and Steve. Went out for dinner. We then went back to the flat.

Bill left today
Awful

Tuesday 24th April 1984

Today it was cloudy again and I went with Mum to Torremolinos but it started to get sunny again so we went home again. I went on the beach for a while but it was not really worth it because it was so cold. I played tennis with the Spanish guy – Luxs for one hour from 6–7 p.m.. He beat me 6-3. I then played tennis with the Dutch father and beat him 6-3. Dad and Henry watched since they came home that day. Today I stayed in with John at his flat – it was good fun.

Wednesday 25th April 1984

Today the weather was really nice and 1 just stayed out in the sun all day. There were some fit Americans who had just arrived at Maite and they walked on the beach with their fit bodies. I stayed with John and Steve on the beach and they got out a Pedalo which I stayed on for an hour. I stayed on the beach all day until 6.30 p.m. I got really red. I got some colour. Then I played tennis with Dad from 7–8 p.m. Beat him 6-3 and then he beat me 2-1. Then I played with Steve until 8.52 p.m. when I got home I packed and had a shower. My hair has gone blonder. I put "Sun In" on it. Then I saw John and Steve; we went to Maminia and I paid and then on to a disco and then John and I stayed near the beach.

Nice

Thursday 26th April 1984

Today I got up at 9 o'clock and I finished packing. 1 went to see John and Steve and they were asleep in bed. I woke them up and said goodbye. It was a beautiful day today. I got the plane at 12.50 p.m. and arrived in England at 3.15 p.m. It was hot here. Everybody was looking at me at the airport. Got home and found that Gertrude had died. Was extremely upset. I was also upset about leaving John. Ate at home but I am determined to be extremely fit from now on. Tomorrow starving myself. Danny phoned and he wants to see me. Things are looking up. Very upset today anyway.

Friday 27th April 1984

Today was my first day back at school. People told me I was brown. Have tennis on Wednesday at 2.30 – 3.30 p.m. and also coaching on a Wednesday so I am pretty busy. It was a very hot day. After school, I ate quite a lot and then I played tennis with my dad at Alderley Edge. Saw Lynne and Paula there. After tennis I did my unpacking which took quite a long time. I also saw Charlotte at Alderley. I ate quite a lot today.

Saturday 28th April 1984

Today I got up about 10 a.m. I sunbathed and I went to Alderley Edge to see if 1 could play tennis. Saw D. Patterson and he looked super fit. Sunbathed for the rest of the day. Went to see Danny, Tez and Natalie and we went to Blackpool which was fun. Went on beach. I ate candy floss, ice cream, rock and baked beans. It was really good fun. Got back about 1 a.m.

Sunday 29th April 1984

Today I got up quite late. I sat outside all day and did my history essay. I wanted to play tennis but did not in the end. I went to bed quite late.

Monday 30th April 1984

Today I went to school and I had an okay day. I am on cold lunches now. Dad said he would play tennis with me at 5 p.m. but he didn't so I had a binge. Anyway we did play at 7–8 p.m. and I played terribly. Dad beat me 6-1. After that I went to an exercise class from 8–9 p.m. at the Leisure Centre which was quite good. I ate a lot when I got home and did not go to bed until 12.30 a.m.

Chapter 5

May 1984

Tuesday 1st May 1984

Today I went to school late as I was extremely tired. I got through the day okay and played tennis with Tracy after school. I beat her 4-1 but it was very windy indeed and was ridiculous! After this I ate a bit and then played tennis with Dad at Mount Carmel Courts. He beat me 6-2. After this I had a shower and watched Dallas. After Dallas I ate a bit and then 1 watched a Jewish programme and then ate quite a bit more. Went to bed about 11.40 p.m. Very late. 1 can't believe how much I'm eating.

Wednesday 2nd May 1984

Today I got to school and went through four boring lessons. I then had tennis coaching at 12 p.m. with Charles Appelwaite til 12.50 p.m. which was okay. Then had lunch and then I played shit tennis from 2–3.30 p.m. and then I played in the trials from 3.30 til 4.30 p.m. I did not play very well. Anyhow, I got home and watched TV and did anything except work. Then got a phone call from Max Arnold! He was asking me out which was very surprising indeed. We stayed on the phone until 11.30 p.m.

Thursday 3rd May 1984

Today I had school and it was okay. Mrs Freer came to me in General Studies and told me I had greatly improved in my essay writing and that I was getting rather good! This made me want to work a lot harder since this was very nice of her to say so, but it wasn't to work out that way. I had tennis trials at 3.30 – 4.30 p.m. Got train back home. Tried to do my essay but I didn't manage to finish it. Jim Salem phoned me to go out but I told him I had too much work to do. Max phoned me again. I couldn't believe it. He kept me on the phone for ages. Decided to have morning off to finish my essay. Had a binge and also went to bed at 2 o'clock.

Friday 4th May 1984

Today I got up very late. I managed to finish my history essay by 12.30 p.m. but knew that I wouldn't be able to copy it up into neat writing so I had to have the whole day off school. Ate nearly a whole ginger cake! Must work a lot more from now on. Went on the sunbed at 3.30 p.m. Got ready for tennis and went with Dad where David was. I played a doubles game with Cheryl and we won 6-3. Ed Viner was there, Paula, Charlotte, Danny McAlpine and quite a lot more people. Cor! Came home and didn't do any work.

Bum exercises

Saturday 5th May 1984

Today I was late for coaching at 11 a.m. with David but it was quite good fun. I played a game with a boy called Nick who beat me 6-1. Oh dear! I had coaching with David from 1–2 p.m. which was okay but I felt he started to not like me. Then Mum picked me up at 3 p.m. I got home and then played tennis with Dad at 5 p.m. Could have gone to the local disco or to Stuart's house but I didn't. Worked instead.

Sunday 6th May 1984

Today I got up quite late. Mum and Dad went cycling. I did some Pure Maths. Then I cycled to Alderley Edge Cricket Club to play tennis with Cheryl. I beat her 6-3 and 8-6. 1 then called to Granny's to tell her I was staying the night. I got home and then did some work, ate then went to Granny's, watched TV and then went to bed at about 11.30 p.m. Slept okay. Must have been the bed though because I had a lot of tennis dreams!

Monday 7th May 1984

Today I got back from Granny's at 11.30 a.m. Had breakfast. Tidied bedroom. Then did some Pure Maths and then I did some History homework. Did bum exercises. Had lunch then Mum and Dad came home with a lot of junk food which I ate a lot of. Eccles cake, chocolate, flapjack, cream (clotted) etc. I had dinner and watched "Best Sellers", last episode, quite good – 79 Park Avenue it's called. Then went to bed at 11.00 p.m. Phoned Tracy – playing tennis tomorrow.

Tuesday 8th May 1984

Today I got to school and had double Drama which was exceedingly bad – v. boring indeed Then I had the rest of the day which went very slowly indeed. Tracy and I got ready for tennis but unbelievably all the courts were taken. Got home, ate and then did some History. Watched Dallas and did some more History. Not a very good day.

Wednesday 9th May 1984

Today had shower and washed my hair. Got ready to go to Manchester University on a trip. Went there with Debbie, Gillian, Andrea and Julie Sassoon. Got there, had coffee and then had a talk. We had lunch; I had a big Ploughman's Lunch which was really fattening in The Phoenix. Then went to Law Department. Went shopping in town — bought 2 tennis skirts (total £13) plus other bits. Got home at 7.30 p.m. Had dinner then ate a lot after dinner. Bed 11.50 p.m.!

Thursday 10th May 1984

Today, I had school and had a tennis practice at 12 p.m. which was quite good fun and then I got home and 1 had to get started on my European History essay. Of course I had left it until the last night. Anyway I managed to finish this one at 12.30 a.m. and it was absolutely terrible. I wrote it out straight into best. I also watched T.O.T.P. I saw Jenny Mesri today at school and she knows and the whole school knows about Max asking me out and me saying no!

Friday 11th May 1984

Today I had to have a shower and wash my hair before I went to school. Helen B. had asked me to go to Marbella with her at Whit but I had to say no because of my school work. What a shame. Today I was supposed to have school coaching but the coach never turned up. After school we went on sunbed, then went to Alderley for Junior night. Saw Charlotte etc. who was playing a match and Paula, Ed Viner. Spoke to David Petty. Rubbish doubles I played. Got home, ate a lot. Max phoned (4th time) (I said I would think about it whether I would go on a date with him!). Jenny phoned. Tez phoned and invited me out tomorrow to Johnny Chestock's Party. Went to bed pretty late after watching a film. A good film.

Saturday 12th May 1984

Today had a match against Withington at school. I was with Tracy as 2nd Team – 1st Couple. Tracy played terribly and so did I. I won 6-3, lost 6-0 – 6-1. Got home about 12 p.m. Had coaching with David from 1.45 – 2.45 p.m. which was awful – he said I was not confident enough. All staff etc. – Mrs Redfern came after me unfortunately, so people are going to know about me being coached – stayed in tonight and worked for once.

Sunday 13th May 1984

Today I got up at 10 a.m. It was a lovely day but I worked from 11 – 12.30 p.m. and then I sunbathed from 12.30 until 2 p.m. Then I went to play tennis with Paula. Beat her 6-2, 6-3. After this got home at 5 p.m. Listened to music, had shower, ate, watched Dynasty. Went to bed at 11.30 p.m.

Monday 14th May 1984

Today I went to School and I nearly missed the coach. Mrs Freer's last day because she is going to hospital tomorrow. After school we had tennis practice which was quite good fun. At about 7 p.m. I played tennis with Dad, then we went to Safeway where I saw Graeme Noon and Gabe Evans. After this I got home and I had tea. Charlotte and Stu had called round but I wasn't in. Max phoned me and I did some Pure Maths homework. I went to bed very late after a binge on loads of food.

Tuesday 15th May 1984

Today I got to school and the first three lessons I spent in the sick bay because I did not want to do Drama. Then the rest of the day went okay. After school I had a binge, then I did some work. I had a shower. I watched Dallas and it was absolutely brill —* I really love it!!! I did a bit of History homework also. I went to bed around 11 p.m. Monday nights – coaching eight pupils at Beechwood Tennis Club.

Wednesday 16th April 1984

Today I finished my Diane (the tablets to help clear my skin). I got to school on bus, only had two proper lessons. It was awful weather today – rain and cold. Had Tennis at 2.30 p.m. which was in the rain and horrible although I had a good (fake) laugh. Came home 4.30 p.m. Did some Economics with Dad. Did some History European notes. Then I did have a big meal (lots of fruit etc.). Went to bed at 11.40 p.m. Quite a good day, however.

Thursday 17th May 1984

Today I got to school; I had duty. I had double Maths and then tennis practice with everybody. I had double Economics. I got home and watched TV and did a bit of work. I watched T.O.T.P. and had a shower. Max phoned me at 11 p.m. and I told him to pee off. I had a big binge. while watching a film on Channel 4. which was okay but very inevitable.

Friday 18th May 1984

Today I only had one lesson but had to go in. {diagram} of Mr Buckley taking the Register, {diagram} had to get up at 7 a.m. Left school at 12 noon. Dad bought me a Prince Racquet Pro from Gilberts which was the one I had been using on a trial basis. It is excellent – I really love it. Dad and I had a knock-up on our grass court. Then I went to the squad practice at Alderley Edge Cricket Club (A.E.C.C.) to see David. Cheryl and Paula were there also. Left at 5.45 p.m. and went to Katie's house and got a lift to school. It was a match vs parents. I played with Katie, we were 3rd couple, with 3rd (Mrs Hafield, Chris) we lost 6-2, 6-3 against 4th couple, lost 6-5 against 1st couple lost 6-0 against 2nd couple (Sarah Taylor's Mum) lost 6-1 but never enjoyed myself so much. It was fantastic fun. Learnt a lot too. Must get up and volley!! Had a big nosh after. Got home by taxi, took Katie home.

Saturday 19th May 1984

Today I got up at 10 a.m. and sunbathed. It was a lovely day. Then went to A.E.C.C. for coaching at 1.45 – 2.45 p.m. – good fun with David. Then played Cheryl, score 6-3, 3-6. I was quite annoyed. Came home, watched TV, ate a bloody lot. Tez phoned thought about David Patterson (D.P.). Went to bed at 12.00 a.m.

Sunday 20th May 1984

Today I got up at 10 a.m. and I did some Pure Maths. Had breakfast. Then I ate quite a lot but once I got down to doing History around 3 o'clock it was okay. Worked until about 7.30 p.m. Had shower and washed hair. Had dinner then got to do some Economics. Went to bed at 10.30 p.m. I did not play tennis today of course!

Period started

Monday 21st May 1984

Today got the bus to school. Had lots of frees today, although two were taken on duties and I should have only had one! Had to do Fiona Chapman's duty. So I had lunch and then one lesson of History. Had tennis practice at 3.30 – 4.30 p.m. where we practiced lobs. I was with Katy Ghazen. Next, Dad picked me up, got home and had quite a lot to eat (400 calories) Then played tennis on a grass court for 1 hour, 6–7 p.m. Worked from 7–8 p.m. and had dinner; about 300 calories over the limit (1000 per day). Did some more work. Got to bed at 11.30 p.m. Very late.

Tuesday 22nd May 1984

Today I had double Drama which was really boring. Did a documentary on corporal punishment. Had double History and double Maths. Had lunch duty and Max did it with me. Felt extremely ugly and horrible. It was raining today as well. Came home, did some work although very minimal. Watched Dallas and also a film later. "Young Love, First Love" – was crap. Ate a lot in the evening i.e. bread and honey etc. Did not play tennis today.

Wednesday 23rd May 1984

Missed bus, caught train at 8.50 a.m. – was late for school. Had Economics then I had Stats. Then a break and a free in which I did nothing. Then I missed a coaching lesson at 12 o'clock with Charles Appelwaite. I didn't know about it. It was boiling hot today. I went outside to sunbathe today on the field and Max and two friends came up and stayed with me which I did not want. Then Joanne W. came to see Max. I played tennis with Katie, she beat me 5-3. Got train home, sunbathed, ate a bit too much (500 calories). Played tennis with Dad on our court (half hour). Did some work. After dinner ate about 200 calories over my limit – toast, honey, bread. Watched Entertainment USA. Max phoned but I did not break down.

Thursday 24th May 1984

Today we had a meeting with the headmaster about the council which was tres boring. Rest of school was pretty boring as well. Got a postcard from John from Lancaster University – v. pleased to receive word from him. Then I ate quite a lot and I hardly did any work. Mum made a cake and I ate at least half of it!!!! Watched T.O.T.P. and did nothing, went to bed quite late.

Friday 25th May 1984

Today I got home from School at 12 p.m., I only went in for my Pure Maths lesson and was knackered. I spoke to Max at school as well. 1 went with Mum to Argos to buy a personal stereo cassette player. Then I went on the sunbed for an hour. I came home and messed about, then I had a shower and washed my hair. I was really contemplating whether to go to the squad training practice but decided not to go as I would be too late. Went to bed very late – no work (1 am).

Saturday 26th May 1984

Today got up quite late. Got ready for coaching at 1.45–2.45 p.m. Got there late. It was an okay lesson. After, I waited for Dad, but he was late. Could not go to town. Went to Wilmslow. Max and Tez phoned. Went out with Max, Stuart H. and his bird to Quaffers in Stockport, q. good fun. Max was really nice and sweet. Got home about 2.10 a.m. Bed at 3 a.m. No work.

Sunday 27th May 1984

Today got up quite late. Mum and Dad went cycling. Phoned Cheryl to cancel tennis. Max phoned. Julliette phoned as well. I phoned Tez and Ric Michaels phoned me also. Tried to do some Economics but failed to do it. I am going mad because I have got so much work. Went to bed at 1 a.m. I'm in love with David (and Max).

Monday 28th May 1984

Today I got up quite late and I had my breakfast; I then did some Economics revision for about three hours. I played with Cheryl at 4.30 until about 7 p.m. at A.E.C.C. I cycled there and back. When I got home I watched TV. The Montreaux Pop Festival. I had my dinner and felt a bit sick. I had a big surprise tonight. Chaz Cooper came to see me. Dad managed to get him away. He looked quite fit as well. I watched TV for a bit more, did some more Economics and went to bed at 11.30 p.m. (tonight I could have gone to Bennetts with Max but I decided against it). My life is becoming better now as well.

Tuesday 29th May 1984

Today I stayed in all day. It was quite sunny and I worked and sunbathed. I played tennis with Dad at Alderley Edge and he beat me 6-3. It was not very busy. Max phoned me today. Did some History (European) + Economics studying.

Wednesday 30th May 1984

Today, I got up quite late and I did some work. It was really hot today and I sunbathed. I played tennis with Cheryl at 5.30 p.m. It was 6-6 and 6-5 to her. Dad came and watched and said I was not playing aggressive enough. Which I wasn't. After that I had a shower. Studying as follows:
History (European)
Economics
Wrote a letter to John from 12–1 a.m.

Thursday 31st May 1984

Today I got up quite early and 1 did some Economics. After this I sat outside most of the afternoon trying to do some English History. It was not very hot. 1 ate quite a lot. I played tennis with Dad at 5.30 p m. and it was really rubbish. He let me get two games, 6-2. After this I watched T.O.T.P. and also did some English History upstairs after having eaten a lot of fuckin' fattening food!! Went to bed at 11.15 p.m.

Studying:

History (English)

Economics

Chapter 6

June 1984

Friday 1st June 1984

Today I got up early ready to go to town. I got the train and arrived there at 11 a.m. I took my passport pictures. Then I looked around Manchester (saw David Patterson, D.P.) and could not find anything nice, no books, no skirt or anything (some nice things in the Warehouse though). I could not get my calculator either. Came home and got ready for tennis, arrived at 5.45 p.m. where I got a game, lost 4-0 and then played Paula. It rained badly tonight. Got home and phoned Max. Watched TV and ate tonight until quite late.

No revision

Saturday 2nd June 1984

Today I got up and got ready to play with Paula. I was very late for her. Played with her and then had coaching at 1.45–2.45 p.m. which was tres shit. We paid David £94.50 (he owes us 50p) with Dad. Went to Macclesfield with Mum – bought shoes; £15 and shorts £20 from Wilmslow. Went out with Max. Went to Mark Whelan's house. Had drinks, watched

Duran Duran video etc. Went to Max J's house and went home at 1 a.m.

Sunday 3rd June 1984

Today 1 woke up at 12.06 p.m. I had breakfast and then I sat outside until 3.30 p.m. reading my English History notes. I then went upstairs to do some proper revision. I did quite a lot of English History until 6 p.m. I then went to the Wilmslow Leisure Centre for one hour on the sunbed. Came home. Max phoned. Had dinner. Did some English History and I got organised for school and tennis after.

Monday 4th June 1984

Today I got to school and I had my medical. Then I went to the library and saw Max. I had Economics. Then I went outside. 1 had a History and Economics lesson in the afternoon. Tennis practice was cancelled so had to wait until 5 o'clock for Mum. I was v. annoyed. I did some Economics revision tonight though I did not do that much.

Tuesday 5th June 1984

Today, I went to school later because of my sty in my eye. I had double History and in the afternoon I had double Maths. When Dad picked me up we went to Safeway's shopping, bought a lot of rubbish, then I went home and I ate it all. I started some Pure Maths and I did chapter 1. That's all I did as well. Charlotte phoned me about a French holiday and I was quite excited (in August). I went to bed at 12 o'clock. Late as usual. Ate badly today.

Wednesday 6th June 1984

Today I had three lessons. I had tennis coaching with Charles Applewaite at school and he taught us how to volley – he was pretty good as well. Then I had a duty which I really did not have but I did in stupidity, then I had tennis, a rubbish doubles but then I played with Katie which was quite good. Walked home with Max, had something to eat, before he drove me home. We then walked to my house from Ned Yates. Charlotte came to see me, we had a good chat. Then I ate quite a lot, muesli etc. and I also played twenty minutes of tennis with my dad and I did chapter 2 of Pure Maths.

Thursday 7th June 1984

Today I went to school and I didn't have a tennis practice. I came home from school and played tennis with Dad for a while. I talked to Max at lunchtime. I did not do any work today, when I say work I mean revision. I watched T.O.T.P., had a shower. I also watched something else after T.O.T.P.

Friday 8th June 1984

Today I did not go to school, went to Doctor August at 11.30 a.m. and he gave me some more Diane for my skin. After this I came home and sat outside to do some revision (European History) but I did not do that much because it was bloody boiling. I decided not to go to tennis at Alderley Edge because I played at home with Henry, Mum and Dad. Henry stayed the night. Had a big nosh up for dinner which was okay. Went to bed really late as I watched a shit film called "Straight on til Morning". Bed 12.45 a.m.

Saturday 9th June 1984

Today I had a match at school vs Dean Row. Played with Grade. Lost 5-6, 3-6 (1 hour). It was extremely close. I then went to Wilmslow with Mum. Also had lesson with Dave which was okay. I had two spots on my face. Lauren Love came round for tennis. Moved into flat above Dad's office by 10.20 p.m. Stayed here, got it sorted out etc.

Started Diane

Sunday 10th June 1984

Today I got up at 7.45 a.m. I had my breakfast and I think I started revising about 9 o'clock. Mum and Dad came round before cycling. I worked a great deal doing European History. I had lunch. I went for a walk at 4 until 6 p.m. I did some more European History. I phoned Charlotte but she was not in. I went to bed about 11.30 p.m. Read in bed. Ate quite a big dinner i.e. a lot of fruit.

Monday 11th June 1984

Today I went to school and it was pretty boring. History was okay. Revising for exams. After this, went home then went shopping to Sainsbury's. Back home, could not revise so I phoned David up to tell him I could not have a lesson this week. We had quite a good chat.

Tuesday 12th June 1984

Today I went to school again so that I didn't miss double History or double Maths for that matter. The exams are coming too quick and I have not revised enough work. I forgot how to revise tonight at my flat! Advantages of studying in the flat in Wilmslow: No TV, no radio, no lots of different rooms to slop in, no distractions i.e. telephone for me, no kitchen and no food to binge, I do not have to revise and no late nights watching TV!

Wednesday 13th June 1984

Today I just went into school for the morning lessons. I bowed out of sports quite successfully as I was on the absentee list as I came in late, having missed the 8.20 a.m. train. Anyway, got home (i.e. the flat in Wilmslow) and revised. Oh, how I hate revising.

I am writing this day on June 27th because I did not find any time during my exams to write my diary.

Thursday 14th June 1984

Today, I took the day off school and revised my Economics and my European History. I did not know my European History very well —> I had only learnt the following topics well by today France 1661–1718 or to the end of Louis XIV, nearly all of Sweden and that's it! I did not learn the Thirty Years War or Brandenburg. Economics is much less to learn and I grasped the Theory of Distribution quite well. Went to bed very late indeed.

Friday 15th June 1984

Morning – Economics I Exam
Afternoon – European History Exam

Today, I had Economics in the morning (2/2 hours). It was three essays and luckily I could do three essays on the paper pretty well. Looking back that was rather an easy paper compared to the rest, I must admit. European History was awful, there was too much choice. I was flummoxed. There were piles of questions on France. I didn't know which one to choose. It was a nightmare (2 hours). I did three shit essays and realised at the end I should have done a good Sweden one which I knew very well instead of a Colbert one.

Saturday 16th June 1984

Last night I slopped around at home, ate a lot, watched TV until the early hours of the morning! This morning I had a match against Sale played with Tracy Munroe and lost two, ate a lot of biscuits. Tracy did not give me a lift home, got home and did absolutely nil revision. Extremely annoyed with myself as I couldn't study because of looking out of my window all the time to see the people.

Sunday 17th June 1984

Today I got up early and tried to revise some English History. I also did some Pure Maths and I did not do any Economics. I was getting rather worked up because I've hardly done any English History or Pure Maths.

Monday 18th June 1984

Today 1 went to school and it was okay because I only had two lessons – Economics and History with Mr Scaife. When 1 got home I revised and I went to Safeway. When I came back I saw David Patterson in his car about 8.10 p.m. He came in, had a pure apple juice drink. We had quite a good chat for about one hour and then he went. I couldn't revise after that. I really do fancy David like mad.

Tuesday 19th June 1984

Today I went to school again, I had Drama. Then I had double History and double Maths. I got home and tried to do some revision. I did mostly Pure Maths but I also did about an hour of Economics. Mummy brought me some exam papers which were not all that helpful. I went to bed extremely late as well.

Wednesday 20th June 1984

Pure Maths Exam
Economics II Exam
This morning I had a Pure Maths exam (3 hours). I thought it was okay although I could not do a few questions but apart from that I thought that I did all right. I was to be surprised. After this exam I went to Broomfield and I tried to revise some Economics and I also bought a lot of sweets to congratulate myself on Maths. I then had Economics – multiple choice was okay but the next part I could not understand so I did terribly in that. Tonight I revised for my English History but not very successfully.

Thursday 21st June 1984

English History Exam (morning)
This morning I woke up at 6 o'clock to revise my English History. I had the exam and of course I was pushed for time. I did not finish the last question and my essays weren't too

cool, so all in all, I did shit. So then after this I went home and relaxed and did fuck all.

John phoned me from L.A.

Friday 22nd June 1984

Today I relaxed at home and did no revision. Oh, actually in fact, I did do some Stats but very little indeed. This was because Dad asked me to do it. I stayed up very late of course and ate a lot.

Saturday 23rd June 1984

Today I had a match at school against Dean Row. I played with Katie. We won one and lost one. (1 hour). It was quite good fun. Then I had coaching which I was late for. David gave me a lift home. Then I walked home and got stung by something vicious, it absolutely killed me.

Sunday 24th June 1984

Today I woke up itching my hand like mad. I was in agony. I tried to do some revision but unsuccessfully. My hand was annoying me, I couldn't even hold my pen. My hand got worse as the day went along.

Monday 25th June 1984

Today after a sleepless night, my hand was a terrible mess. It was all swollen up so Dad phoned Miss Pilkington and she tried to be helpful. I'm sure she didn't believe me. I couldn't do hardly any revision today except looking at my Maths and getting worried. I went to the doctor's and she gave me some tablets, I took one and my sting went down completely. I was really chuffed but I decided today that I would not go to school tomorrow.

Tuesday 26th June 1984

Statistics, Maths Exam (morning)
(+ Afternoon Duty)
Today I did not go to school and so I missed the Stats exam in the morning. I revised of course nearly all day, although I was getting rather worked up because I thought I did not know enough because I found a very large section of Stats which I had not revised before. Oh dear! I tried to get to bed early. Max phoned me.

Wednesday 27th June 1984

Today I went to school and I did my Stats exam (3 hours) in Broomfield with another boy doing a special paper. He smelt the whole room out. It was hard to get into the exam but I think I did okay in the end. After it was over I was so pleased. The end of my exams, hooray! Mum picked me up and I just ate all afternoon. I was in quite a good mood. Today I went to an exercise class from 6.30 – 7.30 p.m.

Thursday 28th June 1984

Today I went to School. Exam results.

I got – Maths Pure 56/2 / 120	Julliette got – 52/2
Maths Stats 82/109	Julliette got – 86
	Overall 69%
Economics = 64%	Julliette got – 57%
History Europe = 68%	Julliette got – 78%
History English = 56%	Julliette got – 62%
Overall = 63%	Overall = 69%

So Julliette beat me in the History by a big amount and I beat her in Economics by a small amount. Julliette is my best friend, but I'm very competitive with her.

Friday 29th June 1984

Today I went into school late for my Pure Maths at 11.20 a.m. I was at my flat today and last night. Dad took me to school which was really nice. After my history lesson I decided to go home. I didn't go to tennis because it was horrible weather. I think it was the last of the squad training course. I watched a really good film, eating a fuckin' great deal of food. It was called "The Cracked Factory" with Natalie Wood. It was about an alcoholic mother – bloody brill. I cried at the end.

Saturday 30th June 1984

Today I got up really late. There was a match at school but I was reserve and I wasn't chosen. I was quite upset. Katie played with Tracy. I had a coaching lesson with David

Patterson which I was very late for – about fifteen minutes. It was a good lesson. Went into Knutsford with Mum and I bought a skirt (£27). I went home and then I went with Max to Jo Ingleby's party which was quite good. Saw a lot of people. I also played tennis today at the grass court.

1 hour studying Economics.

Chapter 7

July 1984

Sunday 1st July 1984

Today I played tennis with Cheryl at 11.30 a.m. She beat me 6-3, 6-4. I then saw Paula, Katie and her sister Simone. We played doubles and we beat them 6-3, 6-0. It was great fun. I got home and I went for a walk and I got a lift to the flat in Wilmslow where I'm studying.

Monday 2nd July 1984

Today I went to school. We had double Economics which was dead boring. Then we had a history lesson going over the exam paper. 1 got home to my flat, I had a session on the sunbed and then I went to Safeway. I got a packet of biscuits because I was expecting D. Patterson to come around. I waited for ages but of course he did not come – what a shame!!! I was invited to a party at Bennetts. It was Raquel's and Mel's but I did not go but Max went. Apparently, he stripped completely. I was disgusted. I found out on Tuesday. I watched Wimbledon and then went home.

Tuesday 3rd July 1984

Today I went to school and had double Drama and then double History and then I had double Maths. Today I went home and I ate about six scones which Mum had made. I played tennis with Daddy for about forty-five minutes. I went to the flat for a couple of things which I needed for the trip tomorrow (a history trip). Went to bed quite late tonight.

* *(very hot today) Started my period today*

Wednesday 4th July 1984

Today I had to get up at 6.50 a.m. I washed my hair and I got ready to go on the History trip. I had to make the taxi driver wait. I sat with Rob Hill on the coach and we had quite a good chat. We stopped at a motorway cafe. We went to Castle Howard at 11.30 til 1.30 p.m. It was really lovely and we looked around the house and the gardens. I was with Sue, Kathleen, Andrea and Julliette. We had lunch, then we went to York where I've been before with a Mount Carmel trip to York Minster and Castle Museum. With Julliette, Kathleen and Andrea we walked around all the shops, eating constantly, had tea. It was okay and fun. Got the coach back with Rob and it was good fun. Got train back, went to flat and went to bed after Wimbledon. *Very hot today.*

Mum and Dad – went to Ireland on bikes

Thursday 5th July 1984

Today, I went to school and I had double Maths and also double Economics. It was very hot today. I went to Alderley Edge to play tennis with Cheryl. I saw Debbie Fletcher and David Patterson who Debbie had a lesson with. I beat Cheryl 6-1 and she beat me 7-5. It was very hot indeed. I also saw Tez and Ed Viner playing tennis. I phoned Ivan to pick me up, went to flat, got things and came home and I ate a great deal. Yesterday I was invited to Jenny Mesri's Party. I decided not to go. Then Jenny phoned me tonight at 9 p.m., we had another chat. (John phoned me from L.A.)

Friday 6th July 1984

Today I decided not to go to school because I only had one lesson so I woke up quite late and had a big breakfast. I was eating constantly all day even though it got quite hot at 12.30 p.m. I sunbathed listening to the Wimbledon semi-finals where Connor beat Lendl and McEnroe beat Pat Cash (Australian). I had six buns today. My tummy was completely bulged. Rick persuaded me to come to his party. Got a taxi to Cheadle Huhne. Bunny picked me up. It was shit, really shit. Bunny gave me a lift to Ned Yates. I walked home. Went to bed at 12.40 a.m.

Saturday 7th July 1984

I am on a diet from today onwards. Today I woke up and got ready for my coaching. I had it for one hour. Then I played tennis with Max from 7–9 p.m. He beat me. It was very hot today. I did not go out tonight, although I could have gone out.

1 hour studying Economics.

Sunday 8th July 1984

Today it got sunny about 12.20 p.m. I sunbathed all afternoon, eating six chocolate cakes and I went to play tennis with Cheryl at 5.30 p.m. We played two sets and I beat her two sets to one. It was Fun Day at the club and there were quite a lot of cute boys there i.e. Mike Hempstock, John Harari, Jim McAlpine etc.

Monday 9th July 1984

Today I went to school and I had double Economics and one lesson of History. I got a lift with Ian McCormick and William to Alderley Edge Cricket Club (A.E.C.C.) and gorgeous, nice, kind, sweet, clever Ian bought me an ice cream. I waited for Paula while watching Brinn Jones playing with Ollie. I then played with Paula and it was one set all. I beat her 6-1 and 4-6. I then got a lift home from Ivan and did not do any work today. Mum and Dad came home from Ireland. I ate a lot today.

Tuesday 10th July 1984

Today I had to go to school. I had double Drama and double History and double Maths. It was an awfully long day. I got home and played tennis with Dad around 7 p.m. It was pretty rubbish. He beat me 6-2. I then went home and I did some Pure Maths corrections today from Debbie Hymen's Maths paper. Yesterday there was a disco at Tiffany's which I did not go to.

Wednesday 11th July 1984

Today it was the last day of school. We had Economics and Maths, we then all got our reports back. I was quite pleased with mine. Julliette and me then went into Cheadle Hulme and had a cup of tea – it was ace, really ace. I ate a lot of fattening cake. Then we went to the Careers Room. Then we got back our reports and read each other's and unfortunately rain got on mine and bloody fuckin' blotted it and spoilt it. Was I pissed off? Yes, I was! I got home after final assembly and then I went to play Brinn which was okay apart from when it rained and we had to stop.

Thursday 12th July 1984

Today I got up quite late but I had to go to school. I wanted to see Mr Welton about my career. We had a good one hour chat about universities etc. and I said that I wanted to start a debating society which gave me a bit of ammunition. Then I got home and ate quite a bit. I played tennis with Brinn for about 1 1/4 an hour which was tres shit. Then I got talking to Rick at the club and there was a cricket match between Cheadle Hulme School and Alderley Edge. There were millions of people from my school. Rick invited me to Bennetts but I didn't go. I felt a real mess today.

Friday 13th July 1984

Today I woke up at 12 o'clock. I had something to eat (quite a lot), then I tidied my bedroom, watched TV and just generally slouched around. Tez phoned me and I think I will be seeing him tomorrow. I went to Alderley Edge to play with Cheryl and I beat her 7-5. There was a nice boy playing tennis with Rick Harari, cor! David Patterson (my tennis coach) of course was here looking tres fit. I went home and then I went a short cycle ride in Mobberley. Watched TV until about 11.30 p.m. and went to bed after writing diary at 12.30 a.m.

Saturday 14th July 1984

Today I had a coaching lesson of one hour with David and we did backhands. Tez and Ed were there. I then played with Paula and I beat her 6-3, 6-3. We then played mixed doubles with Ollie Holt and Richard Harari. I won 6-4, 6-4, swapped partners. I went home and went out with Tez, Ed and friend (Ollie). I went to Stuart Mark's party and saw Ali, Anthony, Johnny Lewis, Neil, Mark Hanburger. Tez gave me a lift home.

1 hour studying pure Maths with Statistics (Stats)

Sunday 15th July 1984

Today I woke up at 1.30 p.m. seeing as I hardly had any sleep with Paula (my friend) sitting outside my door nearly all morning. I played singles with Simone Ghazanfar. Beat her 7-5, 3-1. Played doubles with Cheryl and Paula. We lost 7-6. I got a lift home with Diane Jones and David Johnstone in a really posy car. I went home and ate quite a lot and Weetabix. Went to bed about 12 a.m.

Monday 16th July 1984

Today I woke up at 9.45 a.m. and the cleaner woman came from 10–12 p.m. I got ready to go to Alderley Edge Cricket Club (A.E.C.C.) for the tennis tournament. I had a knock up with Ed Viner and then I had my match with L. Barker and I lost 6-1, 6-2. She was a very soft player and I could not play my hard shots with her, she lobbed me as I rushed to get her diddy shots and she did about ten drop shots. Ed lost, Paula lost, Cheryl won and I met my mixed partner Paul Fosbury who is extremely fit and quite good at tennis. I had a single with him. I beat him 7-6. Went home, watched TV. Ate quite a bit.

Tuesday 17th July 1984

Today I did not have a match. I messed about the house then I got a taxi to Wilmslow to Gilbert's where I bought four balls and some socks (£6.95). I then went to Safeway's and then to Alderley Edge Cricket Club (A.E.C.C.) where 1 played mixed doubles with Paul and Vicky A. and Ed Viner. They beat us by three sets. I then had a drink and stayed at the Club until 8.30 p.m. with Paul. I then went home and ate a lot.

Wednesday 18th July 1984

Today I got up at 10 a.m. and got ready to go to the club for 12 p.m. I played mixed doubles with Paul and then I played girl's doubles – Sally, Paula and we beat them 6-0 and 6-4. It was good fun.

Then I had my mixed doubles with Paul against Ed and Nicky Fowler. They beat us 6-4 and 6-2. It was an awful match (I can't play good tennis on grass. I'm absolutely terrible). Anyway left the Club early and ate a lot when I got home. Went to bed at 1 a.m.

Thursday 19th July 1984

Today it was very hot. I sunbathed then I had a shower and washed my hair and then I went to the cricket club. I saw a girl's doubles between L. Barker, V. Actor and Cheryl and Nicky Fowler. They lost. Then I played tennis with Nicky on grass. She beat me 6-1 and 6-2. Then I went home and I watched TV and ate quite a lot.

Friday 20th July 1984

Today it was the finals at the Alderley Edge Cricket Club (A.E.C.C.). I went at 1.30 p.m. Had picture taken by Express. In the singles Ollie Holt won over Antony Wells and in boy's doubles O. Holt and Brinn beat Paul F. (my mixed partner) and Ed Viner. In girls singles Sally beat Nicky Fowler then came my girl's doubles. I was very nervous indeed. Hardly had a knock up and I was very nervous. It was awful. I played shit and spoilt Sally's chance. Then mixed – Brinn and Sally. Sally won. Ed and Nicky. I was depressed all today. I cried. I felt awful. Tonight I went out and about with Paul and Ivan to the pubs – The Plough, Bull and Brookies. Went to bed late.

Saturday 21st July 1984

Today I cycled to coaching with Dave at 10–11 a.m. Then came home and ate, then went on a cycle ride with Paul over Nether Alderley. It was quite good fun. Then went to the club (A.E.C.C.) to play Vikki. She beat me 7-5 and 6-0! I messed around at the club and went home around 9.30 p.m. Watched TV and then I went to bed. Rick phoned me today.

Sunday 22nd July 1984

Today I got up quite late and I sunbathed and I also played a little tennis. I saw Bobby Braka from New York (N.Y.) and Rob Lever. Then I went to play tennis with Cheryl at 4 p.m. She beat me 6-5, 6-4 then I played a women's doubles. I had a drink with Annabelle my partner and talked to Roger who fancies me. Went home and ate quite a lot tonight. Dad came home.

Monday 23rd July 1984

Today it was very hot so I sunbathed all day, I also did a Jane Fonda workout and went on a cycle ride to Knutsford and then walked around Tatton Park. I could not go through Tatton Park because I did not have the admission fee and a stupid bitch wouldn't let me in for free. I played tennis on the lawn at home afterwards.

Tuesday 24th July 1984

Today I did the Jane Fonda workout. Then with Mum went to Knutsford to Beau Geste. We spent £97 on In Wear clothes. It took ages to choose. We then went home. It was absolutely boiling today but I had missed most of the sun. Paul came round and so did the Lever boys – Robert and Quentin. We all played doubles.

Wednesday 25th July 1984

Today I did the Jane Fonda workout. I went to Manchester. I met Ric Michaels outside Kendals and we had a cup of coffee at a very nice place on King Street. Then we went to the Royal

Exchange. We saw Stuart Hawkswood and his girlfriend, I then did some shopping which was relatively successful in that I bought both shoes and clothes for the holidays. Came back, watched TV and then went to bed.

Thursday 26th July 1984

Today it was not really sunny. I had a very sore throat and cold which was annoying me. I went to Wilmslow with Mum around 3 p.m. and we bought quite a lot of things – a bikini – (£8) from In Wear. We went to the library. Came home and Quentin and Rob were playing tennis. Also Martin had come home from Israel for good. Max phoned. Samantha Spink also came round to see me. She is up here for two weeks. We played doubles for an hour.

Friday 27th July 1984

Today it was the plane flight to Malaga, Spain. We went to the airport. I had a very sore throat and cold and I felt bloody awful. On the plane I had a seat next to two men. One – David – Jewish next to me lives in Wilmslow and Ray who lives in town. We had a really good laugh on the plane, messing about like mad, both had a great sense of humour. It was really good. Apart from me having ear ache. Got to the flat in Spain, walked on the beach and I stayed in tonight. Bobby was also here tonight, has to go cycling with Dad. I did my exercises over a long period of time because I was bored and I also had a very bad sleepless night.

Saturday 28th July 1984

Today I went swimming then went on the beach and spoke to Paco. Got a burnt back! I posed around, got some food, ate quite a lot today i.e. of bread. Which was bad. I exercised at night. I washed my hair. Altogether it was quite a rubbish day. I really do want to see David and Ray in Marbella.

* Period started

Sunday 29th July 1984

Today I went to the beach again but I decided to get less sun (also my bum was burnt). I fancied a fit English lad who has a girlfriend. Also I went to disco, met lots of English girls and nice one called Belle and I got a lot of looks from Spanish boys. All through the night I danced a great deal at the disco. I had a really good time.

Monday 30th July 1984

Today I went to the beach again and I got to know some English lads from Manchester. I also got talking to some girls from Wales. They were all really nice and good fun. I tried to stay out of the sun when it was really hot. I also found out today that Ricardo was here (my Italian summer love). He looked tres fit as well. I met Belle at 10 p.m. but I told her that I was not allowed out because I did not really feel up to it. Felt a little depressed because I was missing out on all the fun but something is bound to turn up tomorrow!!!!!! I hope so – I hope it's Ricardo.

Tuesday 31st July 1984

Today I went to the beach, 1 think for most of the day. At about lunch time I went to the bar and I saw Ricardo and he was quite nice to me. Tonight I went out with my English friends – Belle, Julie, Lorraine. We all went to Malbella II Bar. I saw Ricardo. He was quite nice to me apart from saying he did not like me fat. Then I had quite a good disco night. Saw Paul at the disco.

Chapter 8

August 1984

Wednesday 1st August 1984

Today I went to the beach again. Saw Ricardo for a while. I didn't speak to him though. I went to the disco – Rich, tonight and went with a Spanish boy? I went on his moped which was good fun. I saw Ricardo for a bit tonight and he looked gorgeous – really beautiful and stylish. Went to bed about 3 o'clock. I also saw all my friends on the beach i.e. Matthew from Suffolk, Danny, Lorraine, Julie and Claire, Christine.

Thursday 2nd August 1984

Today I went to the beach again and I was extremely bored. I went out to Malbella II Bar and saw Ricardo who looked gorgeous, tres fit Mmmmmmmm! I also saw Terry and his friends but I decided not to go out because I was too tired.

Friday 3rd August 1984

Today I went on to a beach for the morning and I saw Claire and Christine. I left the beach quite early and got a taxi to meet Charlotte at Malaga Airport. The taxi driver was a real creep and Charlotte said he had a stain on his trousers. Fuck!

Charlotte came home. We unpacked and then I showed Charlotte around the place. We decided to both go on a diet and we did some exercises together which was fun. Then we went to bed about 12 a.m.

Saturday 4th August 1984

Today we went on the beach (Charlotte and me) and then we met Christine and Claire and some boys, we stayed on the beach most of the day. We did some exercises. I talked to this very fit boy (but unsure? I don't know, read on!) Tonight we went to Malbella II Bar with Louis and then we went to Benalmadena to the Chalet and Valentino's and a pub.

Sunday 5th August 1984

Today Charlotte and I went on the beach although it was not as hot as it had been yesterday. We did some exercises and I forget what we did at night time.

Monday 6th August 1984

Today Charlotte and I went on the beach and we sunbathed, although it was not very good weather. Charlotte is dieting and she is losing a lot of weight because she is hardly eating a thing. I am jealous of course because I love eating. Tonight we went to Tivoli World. At first Charlotte and me were not getting on, then we sorted it out and went on Big Wheel, Roller Coaster, The Big Spire and lots of other rides. It was great fun! We had an ice cream and chips. We came home about 2 a.m.

Tuesday 7th August 1984

Today Charlotte and I went on the beach again. I keep on trying to see Paul though not much is happening. Ah! Charlotte is very brown but she does not think so. Tonight we just went out to Malbella II bar and then to Disco Rich. We were with Louise and Mum and Dad had gone out for the night and day cycling and invited Louise back to the Flat. It was very exciting tonight. Saw Paul all by himself, all alone. Just said "hello".

Wednesday 8th August 1984

Today Charlotte and I went to the beach again and I saw Paul and Mark on the Lilo a couple of times on the waves. I really am in love with Paul. He has the most amazing body. He is a professional dancer. Charlotte and I went to Benalmadena tonight to do some shopping. Charlotte bought presents and I bought some jewellery. We had an early night tonight as we were tired out.

Thursday 9th August 1984

Today Charlotte and I went down to the Beach most of the day. I talked to Paul (very fit boy – dancer, lives in North East of UK) with his girlfriend Maxine. I think I am in love with Paul. Had a long chat with them on the beach and then spoke to some Italian boys. Then Charlotte and I said "goodbye" to Paul and Maxine and Mark (brother of Max). I kissed Paul on his cheek, I gave him my phone number. Went out for dinner with Mum and Dad. Could have gone to a Disco with some Spanish boys but stayed at Disco Rich instead which was fuckin' shit. Ate a lot today.

Friday 10th August 1984

Today Paul went home. I was upset all day. It was not sunny today and Charlotte packed and she left at 3.30 p.m. I sunbathed a bit and saw Dario on the beach with Massemo and his friends Franco, he asked me out. I ate quite a lot today. Got ready to go out. Met Dario at Malbella II bar. Had coffee then I went to Torremolinos. Met his friends. Had a drink. Then went to Foy Disco which was really good. Saw Ricardo with a beautiful blonde and then I went back to Dario's flat for a drink. Home at 4 a.m.

Wore Graffiti Jeans

Saturday 11th August 1984

Today it was terrible weather. The sun hardly came out. The waves in the sea were ginormous, really big. I went in with Lorraine and boyfriend. The waves dragged you under all the time. I was really frightened of the rocks every time underneath then another ginormous wave came crashing down. Saw Dario on the beach and went for a drink, then at night I wore green skirt. Went to Foy Disco, messed about here and then went back to Dario's.

Sunday 12th August 1984

Today I went on the beach by myself. I saw Ricardo with his girlfriend and Andre. I did some intensive sunbathing to avoid Dario. Then I spoke to Louise and Flora and Simon (English Lon. Luton Airport). Had a good laugh, ate crisps, ice cream, almond cake etc. Then I went to Foy Disco with Dario and Massemo, Andrea, Claudia, Franc-Louis, Roberto. I wore white shorts, felt good. Saw Ricardo and Spanish girl. Went back to Dario's.

Monday 13th August 1984

Today I went on to the beach and 1 sunbathed and then Dario and Massemo came down on the beach and I sunbathed with them. Dario took pictures of me and Massemo was not very well. Then I went home and I ate quite a lot. I read my book (mags) and ate while Mum was on the beach. I felt a real pig. At 11.30 p.m. I met Dario we had a drink in Malbella II bar and then back to his apartment where we dossed around. Got home around 2.30 a.m. Saw Ricardo for split second.

Wore army gear.

Tuesday 14th August 1984

Today I went down on the beach but it was full of shit (the sea) so Mum and I went on a further beach with really nice new sunbeds. About 4 o'clock Dario came down, sunbathed with him and took pictures etc. After beach saw Ricardo and Andre and Ricardo was really nice to me saying I was beautiful etc. He kissed me a lot as well. This evening I went to Foy Disco with Dario after drink at Malbella II bar and saw Ricardo at Foy Disco and then went to long beach Torremolinos where we stopped the car for a while and Dario and me talked. Got home about 3 o'clock.

Wednesday 15th August 1984

Today I went on the beach, then Dario came down to tell me he was going back home to Italy because Massemo was ill. Took pictures and cried and then I said "goodbye". Dario did not look too bloody sad! For the rest of the day sunbathed and then spoke to Louise for a while and then I had my dinner. Anne wanted me to go to Foy Disco but me and Mum did not have any money left. I did a bit of exercise tonight as well. I really fancy Ricardo and want to go with him but I hardly ever see him, worse luck. He so fuckin' fit. Went to bed around 12 a.m.

Thursday 16th August 1984

Today I went on the beach for the whole day. It was quite hot and I read and swam in the sea. When I got back Mum and I went to Fuengirola where I bought a red bikini and also a lovely pair of white shorts which were dead cute (1400 pasetos). Then we got home and Dad was back. I had a bit of a binge, bread, cake, nuts, rice and mayonnaise and felt really, really, full. Then I did my packing and then I had a shower and wrote this diary. I miss Dario quite a bit and really want to see Ricardo before I go.

Friday 17th August 1984

Today I went on the beach and sunbathed from 11 – 2.30 p.m. My last few desperate hours and I got a red face. I said goodbye to Flora and Louise and anybody else and then got the plane where I had a lovely vegetarian meal. Got back home where I ate a lot of course and watched TV etc, I received two postcards from Rick and Julliette.

Saturday 18th August 1984

Today I stayed at home all day and it was dead fuckin' boring. Ate a fuckin' lot as well.

Sunday 19th August 1984

Today I got up at 1 o'clock. I sunbathed for a while and then I went on a cycle ride with Paul, Ivan's friend. We went to Tatton Park and it was a really good laugh. Quite a lot of people were there. It was a lovely day.

Monday 20th August 1984

Today I got up quite late and I ate quite a lot and then I sunbathed for a bit. Then Dad, me and Martin all went for a cycle ride. We went to Great Budworth which is a very old quaint village and we got back about 6 p.m. and of course I stuffed my face. I phoned Charlotte but she was out.

Tuesday 21st August 1984

Today it was very hot indeed. I sunbathed for most of the day and then I had a shower. Then at about 7 o'clock – Paul (the fit bit) from Spain phoned me from where he lives – Billingham near Middlesborough. I was so chuffed he phoned, I really was. We had quite a good chat and he sounded really gorgeous. He said he would meet me on September 10th because I asked him to. Dad came on the phone and stopped our conversation. I was annoyed. Went to Alderley Edge Cricket Club (A.E.C.C.) with Dad and Mum and I saw a few people.

Wednesday 22nd August 1984

Today I didn't do much once again just like me of course and I sunbathed for about half an hour. I finished "First Among Equals" by Jeffrey Archer and started a new book which I hope to finish before I go to France. Went on a cycle ride with Dad. We went to Dunham Massey Park which was very nice but they wouldn't let in bicycles which was a real pain. We had a nice tea there where I stuffed my face. Came back and watched Miss UK and then went to bed and read my book for an hour.

Thursday 23rd August 1984

Today it was really very hot. In the morning I went to Wilmslow to get my photos and also to do shopping needed for my holiday tomorrow. Then I got back and then went for a little cycle ride with Paul, Martin and Ivan. I saw David Patterson coaching at Alderley Edge Cricket Club and had a chat with him. Then after this I did my packing which was very rushed and unorganised. I got to bed about 12 a.m. because I was looking for some photos from last year for Mum which I couldn't find! I also watched a bit of television.

Friday 24th August 1984

Today I woke up at 6.45 a.m., washed my hair and showered. Then I got a taxi at 7.30 a.m. and I was very early at Charlotte's house. Met Anna and got on shitty coach – no toilet, no drinks, really small and dirty and very out of date. It was a bit like a school bus. We read, talked, slept. Watched videos – "Airplane", "The Fog" and one about Alligators which I didn't watch. We ate a lot on the coach. Went on the ferry and then in France to a lovely cafeteria on the motorway. Couldn't get much sleep on the coach even though all three of us had two seats each. It was really bad. I was up at all different times 1, 3, 4, and then 7.15 p.m.

Saturday 25th August 1984

Today still on the coach till 12.30 p.m. I read etc. When we got to the tent we couldn't believe it, it wasn't clean or anything. Terrible facilities, but the toilets were quite clean but everything – showers, toilets, basin all communal. Looked around, went on the beach, to swimming pool as sand storm at the beach. Then went out for a drink at night and a disco. This is after I had stuffed my face with a whole delicious baguette.

Sunday 26th August 1984

Today it was quite hot and we went down to the beach but there were still sand storms so we decided to find a sheltered place. This morning we went to a meeting of all the campers. I have met two girls – Imogen and Alison (eighteen-year-olds). Really nice, they were — three boys opposite us. Hugh and Andy and a few more young people. Everybody is really young here and without parents so was really good fun — I'm learning how to be independent.

Sunny

Monday 27th August 1984

We have met some nice public-School boys as well called Les, Nick, Peter and Rod. They are really gentleman like. Today it was raining and hazy and no sun and we were utterly depressed. We went into the Canet Playa with Alison and Imogen which was interesting and walked back along the Promenade which was pretty. I went to my first Pop Mobility class and I really enjoyed it tremendously. It did me a world of good. Then went to a barbecue held by Inter-Sun which was really good fun. Food, good cheese. I had games, hilarious, and I won pass the parcel.

Not sunny

Tuesday 28th August 1984

Today it rained this morning and we were screaming in our tents like mad women. We were woken up by our next-door neighbours, they speak so loudly. We got up depressed not knowing what to do. We had some lunch and then we went into different people's tents. Went swimming with Alison and Imogen which was good fun and we sunbathed for approximately one minute because the sun would not come out. Tonight we went to Pop Mobility and did piles of floor exercises which nearly killed me. Went to a Cabaret – v. good, then on to a disco on the camp.

Not sunny

Wednesday 29th August 1984

Today it was the first nice day we have had for ages. Charlotte and Anna and I got down to the beach about 1 p.m. and we stayed there til 5 p.m.. The sun was not right out, it was hazy but all caught the sun. I was like a beetroot. Today my legs were killing me but I still decided to go to Pop Mobility with Glen so I did and I was in agony and had to stop in the aerobics part which was a bit upsetting. Glen is the great black instructor with a gorgeous body. After this had a shower and had dinner – baked beans and then went to the shit disco which is full of fourteen-year-olds and stupid French bastards who are really fit with gorgeous clothes.

Sunny

Thursday 30th August 1984

Today we all went on the beach again. On this holiday I have forgotten to write my diary for six days so I have forgotten what I did on the following days from today. Sorry diary! Tonight I know we went to a pancake party. I had four pancakes which were absolutely delicious. Also tonight we went to the disco. Today also, we all went to Pop Mobility with gorgeous Glen and it was really good fun.
Sunny

Friday 31st August 1984

Today Anna and I went to our first wind surfing lesson. It was on the sand with a windsurfer there. We had a rubbish instructor who was French, instead of getting the American instructor called Gregg who is excellent. Anyway I enjoyed my first lesson a great deal. Tonight Imogen, Alison, Anna and me, all went to the cabaret. It was excellent stuff, really entertaining. Glen was excellent he was a really good singer. Went to disco. Today had a little go on the wind surf with Rod and Nick. Today it is Rod, Nick and Peter's last night.

Sunny, no Pop Mobility

Chapter 9

September 1984

Saturday 1st September 1984

Today Anna and I had our wind surfing lesson on the water with Gregg. I stayed on for an hour and managed to get sailing with the sail upright. It was good fun, fell off a lot and bruised all my legs. Said goodbye to all the public-school boys and were glad to see off our next-door neighbours. (The "oh no!" man from the North East.) Went to disco tonight. *Sunny, No Pop Mobility*

Sunday 2nd September 1984

Have met lots of new friends windsurfing, including some quite fit boys. Today I managed to get a free wind surf but I was not very successful because it was quite windy although actually I did manage to get sailing for about two minutes. It was quite nice weather today. Today there was some Pop Mobility and we all went to the groovy disco.

Sunny

Monday 3rd September 1984

Today, I had a wind surfing lesson at 11 a.m. It was quite windy and I was really determined to get my board sailing. Of course I only managed to do this for a few minutes, a nice man tried to help me and he gave me a few tips on how to hold the sail. This morning I also went jogging with Glen. I really, really, fancy him and I can't get him out of my mind. I really went a slow pace though. How embarrassing! Also today I went to Pop Mobility. There was a Miss Inter-Sun at the barbecue and we all went to the disco. Today it was awful weather.

Not sunny

Tuesday 4th September 1984

I have been getting friendly with a French boy over these past few days. I think he is really fit with blonde spiky hair. Lovely body and gorgeous French clothes. But I am too involved with Glen to like him that much. I went jogging but rather unsuccessfully. Went to the beach all day. I did not go windsurfing because it was much too windy. Today we had Pop Mobility but only for about an hour. Went to the cabaret but it was raining really heavy. Went to the disco and saw Glen and I hung around him a lot and also had two slow dances with him which I loved but then he said thanks and fucked off!!!

Sunny, hazy, phoned Mum

Wednesday 5th September 1984

Today it rained all day and I was totally depressed with the weather. It was really windy and the tent blew about terribly. I ate constantly all day, piles and piles of bread etc. and I broke my fuckin' diet. It was really bad weather all day and I was really miserable. I went to Pop Mobility by myself. Love Glen. He's so fuckin' gorgeous. Tonight went to the disco and danced all night. I had quite a good time. I miss Paul and I don't want to go home. No wind surfing.

Thursday 6th September 1984

Today was another really windy day but the sun did come out for a while and I sunbathed on the camp with Alison and Imogen. I did this then I went to the beach for a swim, then I went to Pop Mobility and saw gorgeous Glen but unfortunately, the music went off and we had to stop. Tonight I ate a lot again. Went into the next-door tent and I really scoffed my face; bread, crisps, biscuits etc. all carbohydrates. Tonight I went to the disco and Glen was really awful to me. He ignored me and was awful to me. I was really upset with him.

Friday 7th September 1984

Today it was a sunny day. I did wind surfing from 10–11 a.m. and then I sunbathed. The French boys came on the beach and Eric came back. Got off the beach quite early, then we went to Disco Pop Mobility at 6 p.m. with Glen. It was my last one with him. It was good fun. Tonight I went to the cabaret. It was good. I then went on the disco. I went with Eric and danced. Danced one, then dance with Glen. Spoke to some boys who went windsurfing i.e. Neil etc.

Saturday 8th September 1984

Today we cleared out the tent. I looked for Glen for a photo. I went to the beach. Windsurfed from 12–1 p.m. and then from 2.30–3.30 p.m. Got off the beach and took a picture of Glen. Then got on the coach straight away, it was awful. I thought a lot of Glen on the bus. Could not get any sleep.

Sunday 9th September 1984

On the coach until 12 p.m. and then got ferry. It was a very rough journey and a lot of people were sick. Today I ate a lot, a lot of sweets and I felt totally depressed. Got off the coach at 7 p.m. Max phoned, I did not speak to him. Mum said I was brown.

Monday 10th September 1984

Today I woke up very late and I slopped around the house eating a great deal. I phoned up Dance Studios and at 10.15 a.m. I left for Altrincham. I was twenty-five minutes late for my lesson. Love it. Into it. It was quite good, joined a drama class on Thursday. I got back. Could have gone to a party of Kathryn Levis's but decided not to go as I was too tired. Katie phoned me. Watched "The Elephant Man" on TV – brilliant film.

Tuesday 11th September 1984

Today I got organised for school. I also ate a lot as well. I went to the sun bed which was shit. I went to bed quite late as well. I was going to go on Rock /Jazz class but decided to go tomorrow. It was quite sunny today.

Wednesday 12th September 1984

Today it was my first day back at school. I was very worried about going to school because of the extent of my hair colour. It was very blonde indeed. However, the reaction was varied. Most people were surprised and others said that they did not like it. Two girls thought it was gorgeous. There were no lessons today. After school I had an interview at the Volunteers Bureau with an awful woman. I then went to a dance class which was extremely good. I really enjoyed myself with Michelle Cohen.

Thursday 13th September 1984

Today we had lessons and we met our new Economics teacher – Mrs Waddington who on first impressions seems very efficient and will get us to work hard unlike Mr Chapman (the old Economics teacher). Also I asked Mr Buckley if he would like to start a debating society. After school I had my first driving lesson after having bought a track suit for £32 at Side Kicks. It was quite good although I was extremely rubbish. Then I went to my drama class at Bermonts, from 6–7 p.m. with Mike Wilson. We were doing the 60's theme which was really good apart from getting home. I waited until 8.50 p.m. to get my lift home. I was extremely annoyed.

Friday 14th September 1984

Today I did not want to go to school but of course I need to make myself go. We had a meeting of the Drama Society about the play. Only five girl's parts. After school Mum and I did a lot of shopping. I read a law book which was extremely good. Went to bed extremely late today after watching a film.

Saturday 15th September 1984

Today I got up very late and I slopped around eating. Max phoned me. I also had a driving lesson with Mum which was quite good. Watched Dynasty and a funny film on TV. Ate a lot today. Max asked me to go out with him tonight but I said no.

Sunday 16th September 1984

Today got up late again. Listened to the radio a lot. Read "Emma" by Charlotte Brontë outside. I did a bit of European History. Then I drove to the Leisure Centre for a sun bed (one hour) and then had dinner and went to bed about 11.25 p.m.

Monday 17th September 1984

Today it was school and I think I got through it okay. After school I had another binge. Did no work and I then went to a volunteers' thingy at Handforth with handicapped people. I helped them try to have fun. Played ping pong and listened to music. It was okay. Got back home very late to eat of course.

Tuesday 18th September 1984

Today I went to school again. I've had a lot of duties this week so my dinner hours have been inconveniently taken up. I did not go to dance class today.

Wednesday 19th September 1984

Today I had my first visit to Match Point for my afternoon sport of tennis, it was really good fun. The Tennis Match Point is a lovely place with lots of gorgeous facilities – sun beds etc. After tennis I went home and then I had an exercise – Rock /Jazz class which was good. It had a lot of emphasis on flat backs. We did a dance routine which was good fun, but I felt really fat. Dad, Mum and Martin picked me up, they went out for a meal while I ate in the car.

Thursday 20th September 1984

Today I did not go to school because I wanted to stay at home and catch up with my work. Of course I didn't do a lot of work although I did some maths and also a bit of European History. I drove to the Bermonts Studio for my drama lesson – okay, Read passages of "Oh What A Lovely War". Then went to an aerobics general work out class which was good fun. I sweated a lot. Got home and I think I ate a lot.

Friday 21st September 1984

Today I went to school and I got a lift from Ian McCormack to Wilmslow Library where I stayed until 8 p.m. working – Economics. I only did a bit of work about two hours because I went out to the shops. Got home and had a big Friday slap up meal with Grandma. I watched TV all night to drown my depression.

Saturday 22nd September 1984

Today woke up late, I stayed in all day. Uncle Albert from America came round. Max and Mark invited me out to Blackpool but when I got out – it was fuckin' shit. It was raining – no Blackpool. Drove around for two to four hours and then ended up at the Aligarth home at 12 o'clock.

Sunday 23rd September 1984

Today I had to do my history essay. I locked myself in the Study from 3–7 p.m. to do it. It took ages and it didn't help that Paul kept annoying me. He made me stay up until about 10 p.m. Depressed. Paul phoned me today!

Monday 24th September 1984

Today I went to school then after it I did some Maths with Statistics at home for the test and a little Pure Maths homework. I did not go to my volunteer work because I had my Stats test to learn so I got Dad to tell them I was ill. Also went to Safeway with Dad.

Tuesday 25th September 1984

Today I had my Stats test and it was really easy. Tonight I was meaning to do some work but did not do any. I did a lot of driving. One hour driving lesson with Mum and I also picked up Martin in the car etc.

Wednesday 26th September 1984

Today we went to Match Point. I really enjoyed the tennis. It is New Year's Eve today (the Jewish New Year) and Mum made a meal and Uncle Joe came round. It was a quite good. Uncle Joe had a big discussion on whether a woman's place is in the home. I ate a lot today of course!!!

Thursday 27th September 1984

Today I went to the synagogue and nobody mentioned my blonde hair. I didn't eat a lot today about 1000 calories in all which is good for me. I am determined from now on to go on a fruit and vegetable diet which I think will involve baked beans. I went to Wilmslow with Dad. After I went to Drama Course and also Aerobics class. I felt extremely fat in my class so now I WANT to lose weight. I'm determined to do it. Okay. I saw a really slim model I want to be like her.

I'm not going to the Exercise Studio until 11th October when I expect to weigh 8 1/2 stone.

Friday 28th September 1984

No diary entry.

Saturday 29th September 1984

No diary entry.

Sunday 30th September 1984

This weekend I prepared my speech for the debate on Monday. I also got some help from Daddy on my speech and he gave me some v. good useful tips.

Chapter 10

October 1984

Monday 1st October 1984

Today I was in a Debate on "A Woman's Place Is In The Home". I spoke against the motion with Jo Woodward. All day I had been trying to learn my speech off by heart. Rob Hill, Mark Whelan and Jo all read their speech. Joanne's speech was shit. I was quite nervous in my speech but I had a clear and loud voice and conveyed my argument well. I got a good clap and quite a lot of people agreed with what I had said. We won in the end by a large majority.

Tuesday 2nd October 1984

Today everybody at school was saying how good I had spoken in the debate. They all said I was much better than Joanne and that she had put me second because she thought I would not be able to speak in public. The opposite was true. I was really chuffed and pleased with myself and thought I had got a good name for speaking in public at last. Hooray!

Wednesday 3rd October 1984

No diary entry

Thursday 4th October 1984

Today at school it was my first time in my Drama class. Mr Westbrook said I was really good in the debate and asked if I had ever done it before! I said that I had. Ian McCormack is in this class and I was really pleased because I fancy him like mad. We read from "The Dresser" a really good play about an actor and his dresser. I spoke in it. Afterwards Debbie Huglin said I was really good at acting and asked if I had done it before!!!

Friday 5th October 1984

This evening it was the evening of Yom Kipper in which you had to fast for over a day (no food, no water). Dad and I went to the synagogue and stayed there until the end of the service. I asked God for forgiveness of my sins and to grant me a better future year. After the synagogue service Dad and I went for a walk. We then went home to sleep.

Saturday 6th October 1984

Dad and I went to the synagogue, in fact I went later. We then went home for a while and came back for three hours. We went to Auntie Betty's to break the fast and I ate a great deal of her delicious food i.e. cheese puffs, trifle, brownies, meringues etc. It was really yummy.

Sunday 7th October 1984

I can't remember

Monday 8th October 1984

No diary entry

Tuesday 9th October 1984

No diary entry

Wednesday 10th October 1984

No diary entry

Thursday 11th October 1984

No diary entry

Friday 12th October 1984

Today I had a driving lesson from 4–5 p.m., after school.

Saturday 13th October 1984

Today I stayed at home, eating and watching TV for most of the day. I went out with Max to see "Blame it on Rio" at Tatton which was really funny and good. Afterwards we went to a pub in Cheadle Hulme. I saw quite a lot of people from school i.e. Rob Hill, Mark and Stuart.

Sunday 14th October 1984

Today I got up very late and I mainly took the day up by watching TV and doing some Economics homework for Monday as I had a test that day.

Monday 15th October 1984

Today after school I had a driving lesson at 4–5 p.m. 1 have been learning to drive in manual as it is much better to get it over and done with whilst I am young. After this I came home, and I had to do an Economics essay which took up most of the night as it was quite difficult and I started it quite late.

Tuesday 16th October 1984

Today I went to school and had a full day's work. I came home and got some English History work done. It was document questions which was very hard. It took me quite a long time to finish. I did not get home until 3 p.m. and I went on a cycle ride and then the back way around Alderley past Alderley Edge Cricket Club. Fell off my bike which hurt and I also had to cycle back in the dark – was out for 1 hour 20 minutes.

Wednesday 17th October 1984

Today went to Match Point after four lessons at school and we had great fun in playing mixed doubles in which we changed partners with everybody and played four games. When I got home I was supposed to do some Math Stats but hardly did any because I am a lazy slob!

Thursday 18th October 1984

Today I went to school and the most important things were (1)I had an interview with Mr Firth (Head Master) about my UCLA. It went okay and I stayed in there for thirty minutes. He asked me some hard questions about law and why I wanted to do it —> I replied to see that justice is done etc. Also Miss Pilkington called me to her office and told me off for my teacher's report which said, "I was disorganised and unpunctual." Was very upset indeed! Also after school there was a debate on vivisection which was very good. I voted for the motion that experiment on animals cannot be justified in civilised society. Didn't go to drama.

Friday 19th October 1984

Today I did not go to school. It was Sim Haftarah (another Jewish holiday) today but I was too tired to go to synagogue so I stayed at home all day. (Dad took a pregnancy test but it was negative – thank heavens.) I watched TV nearly all afternoon. Today I was supposed to go for a thirty-minute tennis lesson with Dave Patterson but I did not want to go. Instead Mum and I went to visit a health club in Knutsford which was quite nice. Had a driving lesson from 8–9 p.m. and I watched TV for the rest of the night. Gillian Cohen rang about a disco. I phoned Max.

Saturday 20th October 1984

Today I woke up very late and I ate a lot today as I was very depressed. Watched TV as well nearly all afternoon. At the evening I watched TV again and ate a lot. I watched TV Super Bowls where David Bryant went. I didn't get to bed until 2 a.m.!!!

Sunday 21st October 1984

Today woke up very late indeed. I only had 200 calories today which is very good. 1 did the Jane Fonda Work Out tape (played it on my cassette player) with Mum. Jeremy phoned and we organised a date for Thursday at 1 p.m. outside Finnigan's. I did some European History and some Economics today.

Monday 22nd October 1984

Today I got up at 9 o'clock. I started work at 9.30–11.30 a.m. Then I did a bit of the Jane Fonda Workout with Mum. Had shower and then had driving lesson from 1.30–2.30 p.m. After this I got back to my work and did Economics for Miss Waddington which was really stupid work. In the afternoon I wasted time from 4.30 to 7 p.m. We went to Alderley Edge for Helen's eighteenth birthday present but only got a card. I got ready for Helen's. I got there at 10 p.m. It was okay, a bit boring. I mostly stayed with Ric, Rob Hill and Max. Max and I left at 1 and I didn't get home until 2 a.m. I went with Max and then I went to bed at 2.30 a.m.

Tuesday 23rd October 1984

Today I got up very late indeed. I did my European History essay today as I wanted to get it over and done with. It took me a long time and after it I had a binge which I was very annoyed about and I went to bed extremely late.

Wednesday 24th October 1984

Today I went to Manchester. I went after lunch because I was very lazy. I got there and bought some books from Sherratt & Hughes and Wilshaws. I then bought a bag from Chelsea Girl for school and some things from The Body Shop. I got home quite late. When I got home I had a big binge. I don't actually know why.

Thursday 25th October 1984

Today I got up and got ready to see Jeremy at 1 p.m. We had lunch at Finnigan's and then looked around Wilmslow. We then had another coffee at the cafe on Grove Street. We then went to see Strattons and then we went to Beltons, a cafe shop on Water Lane. I left and got ready for Drama. Drove there but it was cancelled – was really pleased. Got home and watched T.O.T.P. Went down to Cambridge today to see John.

Friday 26th October 1984

Today I got up very early to see Brian Lever at his solicitors office. I arrived there at 11 a.m. I spoke to Brian until 2 p.m. He described the different types of law and the different cases he deals with.

We then walked to the Crown Court and the Magistrates Courts and sat in some of the hearings, not very good as didn't hear the Barrister's Speech. Met one of his barrister friends. Very nice and helpful. I got back for two hours, looked at some cases left by Brian. Had a final chat with Brian who promised to phone me. Went shopping. Went home quite late.

Saturday 27th October 1984

Today I ate all day. I had a driving lesson from 2–3 p.m. and then I watched TV and ate. I did the Jane Fonda Workout. I watched Wigan, news and Halloween and Hawaii 5-0 while eating a great deal of food.

Sunday 28th October 1984

Today I got up very late and watched TV and ate a lot. I did a Jane Fonda Workout and then read some Economics. I wrote my diary. I continued to eat badly for the rest of the day. I had a big tummy when I did my aerobics.

Monday 29th October 1984

Today was my first day back at school after half-term. Did ski exercises. I was late and I missed two lessons, European History and General Studies. For the rest of the day I did a bit of work. I then got a lift back home with Ian McCormack. He was really nice and I think he wants to go out with me! I did some Economics homework for the test tomorrow. Did Jane Fonda Workout tape. I ate really well today. Max and Ric phoned. I hardly watched any TV which is a good sign and I went to bed at 11 p.m.

Tuesday 30th October 1984

Today I did the ski workout again and I was actually early for school. I had the Economics test which I did terribly in and which I really was mad about because if I had read those sheets more carefully I could have done a great deal better. Very annoying. I had a driving lesson today from 4–5 p.m. which I was fifteen minutes late for. I did a bit of Economics and a bit of Pure Maths homework. I also did the Jane Fonda Workout and had a shower, watched the news and went to bed at 11.30 p.m.

Wednesday 31st October 1984

No diary entry.

Chapter 11

November 1984

Thursday 1st November 1984

No diary entry

Friday 2nd November 1984

No diary entry

Saturday 3rd November 1984

Today just slopped around doing nothing whatsoever and I just ate all day. Did hardly any work.

Sunday 4th November 1984

Today I played tennis with Uncle Joe at 8–9 a.m. and it was good apart from the fact that I had a very red face so there. It was good apart from that.

Monday 5th November 1984

Today I went to school and it was okay apart from doing General Studies lesson. I have been eating a lot recently and it's been awful. I didn't improve a lot today either.

Tuesday 6th November 1984

Today went to school again as per usual. Had a Stats test today.

Wednesday 7th November 1984

Today went to Match Point which was good fun. Played with David Williams most of the time.

Thursday 8th November 1984

Today I went to Side Kicks and I got a complimentary ticket to a fashion show that night. Had a driving lesson. Got ready for show after eating nearly a whole loaf of rye bread. At the Leisure Centre went to the show. Saw Tricia Gallagher, Sam Chadwick and Jo Forsyth, it was a brill show. Two really skinny girls plus the boy who does the swimming at the Leisure Centre.

Friday 9th November 1984

Today went to school and talked to Guy Jones who later phoned me and asked me out but I said no. Went with Helen to Weight Training which was quite good but I don't like the man there. He is horrible. Stayed at Helen's a bit. Uncle Lee came round.

Saturday 10th November 1984

No diary entry

Sunday 11th November 1984

No diary entry

(When I'm depressed, I don't write my diary)

Monday 12th November 1984

No diary entry

Tuesday 13th November 1984

No diary entry

Wednesday 14th November 1984

No diary entry

Thursday 15th November 1984

No diary entry

Friday 16th November 1984

No diary entry

Saturday 17th November 1984

No diary entry

Sunday 18th November 1984

No diary entry

Monday 19th November 1984

No diary entry

Tuesday 20th November 1984

No diary entry

(Depressed)

Wednesday 21st November 1984

No diary entry

Thursday 22nd November 1984

No diary entry

Friday 23rd November 1984

No diary entry

Saturday 24th November 1984

No diary entry

Sunday 25th November 1984

No diary entry

Monday 26th November 1984

No diary entry

Wednesday 28th November 1984

No diary entry

Thursday 29th November 1984

No diary entry

Friday 30th November 1984

No diary entry

Chapter 12

December 1984

Depressed

Saturday 1st December 1984

No diary entry

Sunday 2nd December 1984

No diary entry

Monday 3rd December 1984

No diary entry

Tuesday 4th December 1984

No diary entry

Wednesday 5th December 1984

No diary entry

Thursday 6th December 1984

No diary entry

Friday 7th December 1984

No diary entry

Saturday 8th December 1984

No diary entry

Sunday 9th December 1984

No diary entry

Monday 10th December 1984

No diary entry

Tuesday 11th December 1984

No diary entry

Wednesday 12th December 1984

No diary entry

Thursday 13th December 1984

Day off school – preparing for the Bristol University interview.
In bed most of the day.

Friday 14th December 1984

Today I went to Bristol with Mum and Dad. They drove me down there. I got there at 1.40 p.m, which was a bit of a waste of effort as it was a shit talk by present pupils. Then it was my interview at 2.50 p.m. It was not a very nice interview.

Subjects:

Magistrates and Crown Court (differences, formality etc).

When is a person justified in breaking the Law?

Suffragettes etc,

Nazi Law in the Second World War.

Is it good that the Law takes so long?

It was a real horrible interview and I didn't enjoy it at all. It was not a nice beginning to my skiing holiday.

Saturday 15th December 1984

Airport 6.30 a.m.

Lunch 11.30 a.m.

Arrived at Largem.

Stuck in the same room as Sophie Gellford and Helen Lord. Went out to Belle Vue.

Sunday 16th December 1984

First day on the slopes at 3,000 metres high. It was awful in the morning, afternoon better though because I was with more beginners.

Monday 17th December 1984

Learning how to ski.

It is getting more fun!

I think we went down quite a hard slope.

Tuesday 18th December 1984

People and teachers say that I have got good rhythm in my skiing, i.e. I have a natural rhythm for skiing and should carry it on.

Wednesday 19th December 1984

Skiing again.
I am really enjoying it!
I went down – Vorab I think!

Thursday 20th December 1984

I hurt my lip today sledging with Richard Burrows.

Phil Harden	Nigel Harris	Mark Hancock	Ian Burrows	Phil Harden	Nigel Harris	Mark Hancock
Guy	Richard Harris	Simon Ligne	Jason Varey	Guy	Richard Harris	Simon Ligne
Corky	Phillip Fox	Giles Gatford	Fraser	Corky	Phillip Fox	Giles Gatford
Paul	John Nay	Tim Perry	Oliver Jackson	Paul	John Nay	Tim Perry
John Beard	Simon Savage	John Bagshaw	Chris	John Beard	Simon Savage	John Bagshaw
Eddie Beardwell	Matt Savage	Robert Bigs	Rupert	Eddie Beardwell	Matt Savage	Robert Bigs
Michael Harris	Charles Savage (Cor!!)		Nick Constance	Michael Harris	Charles Savage (Cor!!)	

Friday 21st December 1984

Skiing is cold and I wish I had taken better gloves because you can get cold hands quickly. Once you get skiing you warm up quickly.

Saturday 22nd December 1984

Today I was moved up a group and I was really pleased about it because I can ski in a much faster group now.

Sunday 23rd December 1984

Skiing is really brill. Very invigorating. I've come home with a lovely glowing face.

Monday 24th December 1984

I think it was free skiing today. I cut my chin skiing. I fell down on a very steep slope while I was traversing!!!

Tuesday 25th December 1984

Christmas Day
It was really depressing apart from the Christmas lunch and present giving. We had skiing with Andy Davies and also Mr Davies's son. It ended at half day due to bad weather conditions.

Wednesday 26th December 1984

Today it was free skiing. I unfortunately got stuck with Jason Varey and Guy Birch Jones. Morning was okay. I actually enjoyed La Scala. Would you believe it – fell – that was with

Ollie and Chris and Fraser etc. Afternoon was absolutely awful. Jason zooming off posing everywhere.

Thursday 27th December 1984

Today it was home time. I fell sick all day as I had eaten so much. I got a wink off Charles on the plane and two kisses of him when we got to Manchester Airport, cor!

Friday 28th December 1984

No diary entry

Saturday 29th December 1984

No diary entry

Sunday 30th December 1984

No diary entry
Monday 31st December 1984 No diary entry

Exercise Programme

1984

Warm Up

1. Head Rolls
2. Shoulder Lifts
3. Side Stretches (i.e. Lift Arms, Stretch Both Arms)
4. Waist Reaches
5. Hamstring Stretches
6. Hamstring Stretches (Hold ankles for 8)
7. Spine Stretch (Legs bent, hands through legs)
8. Hamstring Stretches (i.e. 4 counts to left, right, centre)
9. Hamstring Stretches (Bent knees, hands on floor, straight legs)
10. Calf Raises (Left calf on bent knees, knees out)
11. Inner Thigh Stretch
12. Roll Up

Aerobics

13. Jog (20), Jumping Jacks (10), Jumping Twists (20), Heels Up (10), Knees Up (10), Jog, Leg Swings (10), Jog (10)
14. Roll Down and Knee Bends (like 9 but legs together)
15. Tendon Stretch (bounce right heel, st. legs)
16. Roll Up and Stretch

Waist

17. Side Pulls (20 to each side pos. with right arm up, left arm to side)
18. More Side Pulls —»8 bounces in each 3 positions.
19. Also Hip Turns to relax.
20. Waist Twists

Buttocks

21. Buttock Lifts:-
a) 10 with legs normal
b) Open Legs, 10 Butt Lifts
c) Knee together and Strength Open Legs, 10 Butt Lifts
d) Rapid Knee Bounces, Buttock Lifts
e) Knees Together, still rapid Lifts of Butt
f) Feet together, 10 Lifts
22. Hip Release and Stretch

Notes and Memoirs

1984

Sunday 29th January 1984

My best friends are:
Samantha Spink (now lives in Devon – September 1983)
Charlotte Wed
Helen Beaumont?
Julliette Franklin?
Jenny Mesri.

I really, really fancy
Danny Shineman
Andrew Kingsley (he is beautiful) – going out with Danielle
Chaz Cooper
Ric Goddard
Philip Copeland
David Patterson
Johnny Morris (London)
Paul Fosbury.

Spanish Exercise Programme
12 – 26th April

1984

1. Touch toes
2. Hands through legs
3. Waist Benders (3 different kinds)
4. Bum Exercises – with point and flex
5. Leg Exercise on floor – with point and flex
6. Different kinds of bust exercises
7. Try and skip every day too, if I have not played Tennis. 200 – 500

Aim:-
To lose ½ stone to get back to 8 stone in the morning – 8½ stone at night.
Instead of 8½ stone in the morning – 9 stone at night.